Dedication

I would like to dedicate this book to my wonderful Lord and Saviour Jesus Christ, who not only gave me life, but protected me and preserved my life during my early childhood. He is the reason I was able to write this book.

I would also like to dedicate this book to all those who are suffering as a result of a broken childhood, praying that the comfort I have received you also will receive through my story.

Acknowledgments

I would like to give a huge thank you, to my precious friends, Barbara Law for all the hard work she has done editing my book, and also I would like to thank Anne Mathews for all the help she has given me while working on this book.

I want to thank my husband Ray for being such a great husband and giving me tremendous support in persevering with the project of writing my story

First Published in 2010 by Rayla Ministries.
71 Lower Dock Street, Newport, South Wales NP20 1EH, UK

ISBN 978-0-9546941-1-1

Designed by: Carol Thomas, Xheight Limited, Newport
Cover Design by: Simon Clement, Kings Church, Newport
Printed by: JF Print Ltd, Somerset

WARNING

This book contains strong language that is necessary to accurately portray the events that took place, but which, to some people, may be offensive. Where such words were spoken in the Norwegian language I have used the English equivalent. I also would like to warn those who may be sensitive to reading about abuse that this book is very graphic and may be traumatic for some to read.

Please Note

With the exception of the author's name and her husband Ray, all the names in this book, including those of pets, have been changed to protect the privacy of the families of others.

A Note from the Author

I started to write this book in January of 2008 and I finished writing my story in August of 2009. At first I was not sure where to start and how I was going to manage to write my story in English, especially as I am Norwegian. I didn't know how much I would remember, and I didn't know if I could put into writing the events that I could recollect. I wanted to tell my story just as it was, so I decided I would begin by writing about just one experience that came to mind, in order to prove to myself that I could in fact express myself in writing. I wanted to write my story as I experienced it, and how I remembered it. I also wanted to write about how I felt and the thoughts that were in my mind as a child. I didn't want to disguise the truth by removing the bad language that was spoken to me. The words were more painful than any of the beatings.

When I had completed the introduction, I put aside the project, trying to convince myself that I would never be able to write the book. Three months later, I knew I had to persevere with the project and continue with my story. I had been totally healed years before from my broken background, and I have preached at many churches, in several countries, about the things I went through to help people realize that there can be a life beyond a broken childhood.

A scar is evidence of a place that once endured pain, and possibly bled, but it doesn't hurt anymore--it's just a mark. I compare my life to a scar. As I tell my story at different church venues around the world, I show people the "scars" in my soul that once bled, the scars that were a result of so much suffering. But during the process of sharing, I had felt none of the pain I felt as a child. I was healed and there was no longer any "blood" or sadness.

I was determined when I started this book that I was not going to just show my scars.

But it became a different journey altogether; it became an emotional rollercoaster! As I penned the facts of what happened to me and how I felt at that time, onto the paper, I felt as if I had physically reopened the scars of my soul once again, allowing them to bleed, feeling the pain from the wounds of the past.

I didn't realize that this extraordinary journey would transport me back in time, where I would actually become a little girl again, not only reliving those years, but also experiencing the exact pain I felt as a child. There were times during the writing when I felt the need to close my laptop and leave the room to find seclusion, where I could just sob and sob. On those days I was happy to be alone in the house. One day I ran into the bathroom, where I started to cry uncontrollably. The pain had become so unbearable that I shouted to God, if He didn't take the pain away, I would not write one more word. I paused for a moment and took in a deep breath. When I cried out to God I suddenly felt a deep peace on the inside that I can not explain with words. The pain that I had felt while typing the passage I had just written left. A thought came into my head: "It will be okay, I will not give you more than you can bear." I knew that thought came from God and I would be able to continue to write. I walked back to my laptop very relieved and continued my work.

Still there were times when I was unable to write anything for weeks at a time, sometimes months. I was scared, as I didn't know what memories would pop up next and how many details I would remember. Other times I felt I was not able to type fast enough because of everything I could remember.

This book is about how I experienced my childhood, how I felt during the abuse, how I survived against the odds, and what effect my childhood has had on my adult life. It tells how a young mum, with a broken background, coped. We all react differently to the various things that happen to us. I have written about how it was for me and how it shaped me as a person, sometimes in a bad way, but how it ended for the good.

I have tried to write my story in the correct order of events, but there may be differences in dates and times of certain happenings.

I hope this book will inspire those who are still living in broken homes and are suffering under abuse, to be encouraged and know that their childhood does not need to dominate them for the rest of their lives--there is a future and a hope. There is a life beyond a stolen childhood!

Stolen Childhood

Introduction

I WAS NOT AFRAID OF DYING
BUT AFRAID OF LIVING

I ran upstairs as fast as I could, to the first floor, then to the attic to where my grandparents' bedroom was. All I could think of was how to escape. "I have to get away, I have to get away" were the thoughts that raced through my mind, as tears ran down my cheeks. It really hurt this time, my brother had beaten me so badly, and whenever he started to beat me, he never wanted to stop. The more he beat me, the worse he got. It was as if he were driven by some morbid satisfaction of knowing what parts on my body to beat to cause the most pain.

He would start by smacking me around the head until I fell to the floor; there he had me in a position that he could really get at me. First the stomach! He would kick and kick until I was forced into a foetal position. Next it was my head. He would grab me by the hair and knock my head like a rag doll on the hard wooden floor. I would feel his nails plunge into my face until the blood flowed. I was in agonizing pain. "Get off me, get off me, you devil!" I screamed. There was no other way I could defend myself, other than using my mouth. But the more I called him a devil, the worse he got.

This time I was in agony in my chest and stomach. I had difficulty breathing - it had been six months now with violence constantly. I could not take it any longer. There was normally a day or two between the beatings and kicking. I looked on that as a kind of respite, to recover at least a little bit before the next onslaught.

My grandparents were in Denmark visiting my aunt and had been away for six months, so they were unable to protect me from the boy I called the "devil," the boy who happened to be my brother. I called him the "devil" because, just before he started the beating, I would see his eyes change. It was as if I could actually see the devil in him. I never even knew there was a devil, but I saw evil in my brother's eyes. I thought that if there was a devil, this must be him. We would play as normal children usually do, then suddenly, out of nowhere and for no reason at all, I would see that look in his eyes, and I knew there would be trouble.

When I entered my grandparents' bedroom I was met with only emptiness. The ceiling was so low in this small room that a very short adult person could reach it, and there was barely enough room for two beds on either side. The beds were separated by a small pathway in between and a tiny window between the beds gave some natural daylight. I ran towards Granny's bed and grabbed her big pillow, searching for something connected with her. I hugged her pillow tightly into my body while I shut my eyes and smelled it. I clung to it, trying to pretend Granny was still there. I fell down on my knees with my arms tightly wrapped around the pillow and shouted, "JESUS! Help me! Help me! Please take me away from this hell, take me away, PLEASE HELP!" I cried out to God sobbing words that I could hardly pronounce--my voice had gone, because of all the crying I had endured for such a long time and also from being surrounded by cigarette smoke day and night.

I stopped in the middle of my prayer, hoping to hear Jesus' voice answer my cry and I waited for a magic wind to lift me up and fly me as far away as possible, to somewhere nice, warm and caring. Surely, Jesus would do that for me--who else could I turn to? I was devastated when nothing came, no sound of His voice, and as I opened my eyes I saw that I was still in the same place. I had not been taken away. The thought that I would still have to face the continual abuse from my brother devastated me. There was also another source of torment that I had to endure, that of the mental abuse and beatings from my father.

The thought of Jesus being silent and not rescuing me from this hell took from me the little faith I had in Him at that time. It was 18 years before I could say a prayer to Jesus again. Something in me just broke. I was alone, I was always alone, no one to run to, nowhere to seek rescue or comfort. That was the cold, hard fact.

The bleak winter afternoon was now getting darker. I slowly got up from my knees, throwing the pillow back on my grandmother's bed. I thought to myself, there is no Jesus, there is no other way to escape, than to end this misery of a life myself.

I put on my light blue coat, one that my mother had sewn for me, and walked out of the house and down the road about 150 meters from the farm. It was very cold and it was snowing heavily. There was about six feet of snow on each side of the road and I found a spot and just sat down like a little bundle in the middle of the road, with my fingers in my ears and my eyes tightly shut waiting for a car to hit me. The visibility in this blizzard was around six feet.

I was eight years old and about to commit suicide. I had lost all hope and I saw no future. I knew it would not be long before it would all be over, no more beatings, no more pain, I would finally escape. This road had a lot of traffic and all I had to do now was to sit and wait, and as I sat there all I could feel was numbness, I had no fear. I was not afraid of dying. I was afraid of living

Chapter 1

THE BEGINNING

My Dad was born in the mid 1930's. For a while he worked on a small fishing boat which sailed up north and docked at many different ports. I have often heard the story of how Mum and Dad met. One day he docked at the port in the city where my Mum came from. In the evening a dance was held at the local community hall. All the men from the fishing boat went to the dance to see if they could chat up some of the local girls. Dad had great experience with women, as he was known as the most handsome man in our valley, and the girls lined up to get a chance with him. With his pitch black hair combed back like Elvis, the women ran like crazy after him. He was the first man to own a motorbike in our county, and he showed off like Steve McQueen. He was also the first young man in the village to own a car, a beautiful Chevrolet!

When Dad entered the community hall, his eyes glanced around the hall and suddenly stopped when he saw the most beautiful girl in the room. Mum was standing there chatting with some of her friends, and Dad put on all his charm and made his way towards her. "Shall we dance"? he asked her. Mum could not believe her own eyes when this handsome hunk of a man asked her for the first dance. They both fell in love at first sight. In the years after Mum's death, Dad would take out his accordion, close his eyes tightly, and then play the very song they had danced to on that first night. He would repeat over and over again, "This was our song, the song we danced to for the first time. It was during this song we fell in love." I struggled as an adult to hear Dad reminiscing after Mum's death, because I saw the pain of regret lingering in his eyes.

Dad came from an idyllic, little farm among the beautiful mountains and fjords in the west of Norway. His parents had always loved him and Granny said he had never gone hungry, even when he was a young boy during the war. He had two sisters that were around his own age and a brother who was born after they had grown up.

Granny used to say that Dad was spoiled because he inherited the farm from his uncle when he was only 9 years old, so everything was really handed to him on a plate. His parents ran the farm for him until he was old enough to handle it himself. At the time they had a few cows, a horse, a pig, goats and some hens.

As a young man, Dad worked as a cook and a fisherman on a small fishing boat to earn some extra money, and he used to go out to sea during the herring season. Granny and Granddad continued to run the farm for him whilst he was at sea. He was really just out on an adventure, waiting to get the confidence to take over the farm.

Mum was only 17 when she married my Dad. This young, pretty 17 year old fell in love with the most handsome man she had ever seen and thought she was heading for a better life, far away from her own home.

Mum had a totally different background and upbringing than my Dad had experienced. Her parents divorced once her childhood was over, but she had grown up knowing immense violence in the home. At one time her father returned home drunk and in a furious rage grabbed his rifle and shot at his wife, my Nan, luckily missing Nan, my Mum, and her sister Wilma. But he would often threaten to shoot them all when he was drinking.

I somehow knew, even when I was very young, that there was something seriously wrong with my Mum's mother. Nan would suddenly shout and yell at voices she claimed that she could hear in the walls. She believed that there were people after her, trying to wire her house, in order to speak to her through microphones, just to torment her. Nan thought there were people out to spy on her, wanting to kill her. Sometimes she thought that someone was putting sulphur in her tap water; consequently, she would go to her neighbours with empty buckets to get drinking water from them.

Nan also thought people were stealing her food, replacing what she had bought with bad food. She thought that they put poison in the fresh food she bought from the supermarket. When Nan went shopping, the shop owner dreaded seeing her, because she would break the seals on the food coverings in order to taste and see if there was anything like sulphur added to the items. It also took her about an hour to pay for the food, because she thought the cashier was stealing money from her, so item by item the cashier had to show Nan that the bill was right.

Often she threw out all her food, like flour, milk, eggs and fruit, onto her outdoor stairway and landing, saying she was showing her neighbours and the world that she had discovered the plot to kill her. She would show them that they hadn't succeeded in their plan because she would not be eating the poisoned food!

The food lay there, in all weathers, until it rotted. As Nan grew more insane, she thought of all the germs that would spread, so she continually scrubbed and cleaned her outdoor stairway and landing until it was sterilized.

Whenever I visited my Nan for a holiday, she showed me the bullet holes in her kitchen walls, evidence of the time her ex-husband tried to kill her, my Mum and her sister Wilma. Nan would repeatedly tell me that her ex-husband wanted to sell her to the Nazis for 24 boxes of beer. She told me how he beat her time and time again. One time he beat her for two and a half hours non-stop and she almost bled to death. Nan recollected the time she was pregnant, but bled so much that she lost the baby and her husband did not even call for a doctor!

When Mum was a child, Nan would force Mum to skive off school and go with her to the prawn factory to help her peel prawns. The more prawns you peeled the greater the wages, so having Mum there helped Nan financially. Of course it was hard times for Nan, just after the war, so she really needed help to make ends meet, especially since her husband was out drinking all the time.

There was a nasty side to Nan though; she would often fake a heart attack, by throwing herself down on the floor, groaning barely, "Help me, I am dying, you can't leave me now." This would happen at key times. For example, the charade would take place just before Mum went to school, then she would have to stay home. Mum never stood up for herself, she just took what Nan gave her, whether it was good or bad. I guess Mum felt she was responsible for taking care of her. I think Nan's manipulation, by faking that she was dying all the time, must have created a deep fear in Mum.

Mum's sister Wilma was totally different. She was five years younger than Mum, and she just ran off and didn't care the least. Wilma had seen through her mum's manipulation. Why then would she need to stay home to look after her mother, when my mum was there?

So when this handsome man came ashore, to the beautiful landscape in the north of Norway and Mum set her eyes on him, she was not going to let him go! Dad had to go back to the boat, but promised to come and get Mum, as soon as he had earned some money and the herring season was over. Mum was happy and excited to have found the love of her life and with an adventurous spirit left home when Dad came back to take her down to the west of Norway, about 600 miles away.

It didn't take long before Mum got pregnant with her first child. She was only 17 but now she had finally escaped from the hell she had grown up in with her mum. Mum was under the legal age of eighteen to get married, so they had to apply to the King of Norway to get permission to marry. When permission was granted, the wedding went ahead, and the wedding party lasted three days. Just three months after their wedding, my oldest sister Mary was born.

Chapter 2

THE LAST BABY

Seven years later, on a cold early Monday morning, 7th February 1966, I was born. I was the fifth child born in seven years. Mary was seven years old when I was born, Sally was six, Angela was four, and Ted was two. Mum must have gone into labour the day before, on my sister's birthday. She never had any problems giving birth to any of her children; the delivery I was told, went well.

The snow always lays thick in the west of Norway, sometimes just overnight it can snow up to two feet and even more. To get out of the house we needed to shovel away the snow that had blown up against the outside door that had fallen overnight. The only way the snow was removed was by hand and only years later, when my brother Ted took over the farm, did they use a tractor.

Very often the snow is over six feet deep in the fields, and it starts to fall around October and stays until the beginning of May. The winter nights are very long and dark. There are not many hours of daylight during the mid winter in Norway. The sun would hide away for three months where we couldn't see it.

It would glide behind the big mountain in front of the house so all we could see was blue sky but not the sun. On the day that I was born there were luckily no weather problems and my parents managed to get through in the car to the hospital, but I still can imagine how difficult it must have been for Mum at this point. She was just 25 years old and now giving birth to her fifth child.

In addition to the challenges of now having five small children, the conditions of my parents' house were very primitive. It was built in 1893 with thick timber logs laid on top of each other and chinked into place at each corner using an old building technique. The outside timber walls had been covered with wall panels that were not painted. The house had lots of windows on each side; each individual window had six small, single panes of glass. The poor quality of these old windows gave away the very little heat there was at any time. There was a kitchen and two living rooms downstairs and one living room and a kitchen upstairs. The one living room downstairs with the dining table was only heated and used for special occasions. When we finally got a TV, the room was turned into a sitting room, and the old windows were changed to a newer type that didn't give away so much of the heat. Then there was a long T-shaped hall which was always freezing cold, with a long, steep stairway with twelve steps that led up to the next floor. The main entrance faced the very busy road, and at the back there was also an entrance to the path up to the barn.

My parents lived in the upstairs part of the house, while Granny and Granddad lived downstairs. In the later years they would swap, and Mum and Dad moved downstairs. Only one room in each apartment would be heated at a time—the living room. The rest of the house was always freezing cold, especially in the wintertime, so when we walked around the rest of the

house, we could see our breath. There was no hot water. Mum
had a big saucepan on the hob that was used to heat water for our
dishes. There was also a big pan used to boil the towels when
they needed washing. It was not until I was older that Mum got a
proper washing machine. This helped a lot, especially when we
had a bath now and again; she then used the washing machine to
heat up the water for the bath. In 1976 we finally had installed a
100 litre hot water tank.

I have, of course, no memories of my first year, only the things
that I have been told. By the time I was born Mum was probably
already very depressed. She hated the place she lived in, hated
the farm, hated the people around her and she could not stand
her mother in-law. She thought she had got the best in-laws in
the world when she married Dad. With Granny's generosity and
her bubbly nature, Mum thought she had arrived in Heaven in
comparison to her own schizophrenic mum. But the view Mum
had of Granny would soon change.

I don't really know what went wrong or what could have
happened for Mum to begin to hate Granny as much as she did,
which later became so bad that I remember Mum saying when
she was drunk that she wanted to see Granny dead. "I hate that
bloody witch, I cannot stand her," she would say. Mum said that
she wanted to see Granny hang on a tree, and then she would light
a fire under the tree and hope she would burn for eternity with
loads of pain. "Then I will stand under the tree," Mum said, "and
laugh and laugh, because that bitch got what she deserved." I
remember Granny used to repeat again and again the horrendous
story of Mum wanting her dead. Of course I always sided with
Granny; how on earth could someone want to kill my Granny?

My guess is that the more kids Mum gave birth to, the more

she could not stay in control. I also think she had growing pressure from Dad. I particularly remember that when he came home from work, he demanded his slippers be put before him when he walked through the door.

Dinner also had to be ready as soon as he came home. Quite often Dad didn't come home at a set time, and Mum would have been starving all day, not eating before dinnertime. Sometimes we would start to eat if Dad hadn't arrived. Then when he arrived, he would be furious and slam the doors and shout and scream till he went into another room where he would pout and feel sorry for himself. And then there were times that Dad came home early and Mum hadn't had time to finish dinner for him yet; then he would react in the same way.

After Dad took over the farm that Granddad and Granny had run for him since he was nine years old, he also had to work to bring in extra money; the farm was so small that it wasn't enough to live off. No matter what Mum did to help Dad, though, it was never good enough. When he was working, Mum had to do the daily chores on the farm—milk the cows and give them food. After milking the cows, she had to put the milk into big buckets and then lower them into a well where the milk was kept cold. I remember her lifting those heavy buckets full of milk, loading our milk wagon and wheeling it down to the road where the milk truck came to pick it up. We had a lot of hens and she picked eggs every morning and fed all of them. All the sheep also needed food and I can vaguely remember that there were some pigs too. After feeding all the cattle she then had to remove all the manure from where the cows were kept. She tended to the whole farm.

She also needed to make sure we had clothes. There was little money so she sewed all of our clothes herself. All her four girls had identical dresses and Ted's trousers always matched the girls' outfits. Mum's mother was very handy and had taught her how to sew. She did an excellent job. She also cooked and baked all our food from scratch. There were endless tasks for her to do. Because of all this and with a bunch of kids running everywhere, she may have become more and more depressed and troubled with her nerves.

By this time, Ted had already found great pleasure in his game of making my life a living hell. So the sound that would go through the whole house was me crying all the time, caused by Ted's daily games. Of course when Granny was home she came to my rescue, because I often ran to her and managed to stay away from Ted.

With all the pressure of the kids adoring Granny and not seeming to care about Mum at all, I think Mum had to find a way an outlet for it all. I think Mum used the fact that she hated Granny as an excuse about how she really hated her own life.

As kids do, they run for comfort to where they can get it and that is often the grandparents, if they live in the same house. When Mum told us off and we ran to Granny, she would side with us and wipe snot and tears off our faces saying words like, "How on earth can your Mum do such things to you, I'll look after you, don't worry." I remember I would feel great after that.

Granny had a fantastic way with kids; she would play and be like a child herself with us. Granny often took out her guitar and started singing and joking with me. I looked at her with admiration and thought she was the best guitar player in the whole world. She sang old folksongs and polkas and little rhymes. I dreamt of getting as good as my Granny on the guitar one day, and then I could be a famous pop star.

Granny made me laugh a lot and I felt she cared and really loved me. She always used to say when I was alone with her; you are the best of all the kids, you are the most special and closest to my heart. Later I found out that she said the same to everyone, and I remember feeling let down because I really thought that I was the best. As an adult I learned that by her saying those things, she made all the kids feel special, because we all really believed it to be true.

The respect we had for our parents was next to nothing. Mum's attempt at getting the kids to be obedient was useless. So in the end I guess Mum gave up trying to try to raise us, because the kids always seem to run to Granny. I also guess that Mum was very jealous of Granny, because it might have appeared that we loved her more. Granny had a way of showing the kids how much she loved them; she said it with her words and also her actions. Granny also had such a way with the kids that we wanted to help her with things and chores. She said things like, "You are such a wonderful and quick kid, I am sure you are able to help Granny with this. Think how good you are, I am so amazed at how clever you are." When Granny spoke in such a way, the kids wanted to prove her right.

I think Mum had no chance of showing us love like that or if she even knew how to show us that she loved us. I think she didn't know how to show love at all. She had lived in fear all her life, and now that she had kids of her own, there was no way of knowing how to show something she had never experienced. Mum thought Granny stole our hearts, and she never forgave her for that.

Mum's arrival at the farm must have been hard. She left home at the age of 17, and moved 600 miles away from her only sister,

Wilma, and though her mum was the way she was, I think she loved her. It couldn't have been easy leaving her alcoholic father either. He lived in a little cabin where he got drunk most of the time, but he was her father and she had a special attachment to him.

When Mum arrived in western Norway she found the house very dirty and there were few separate bedrooms. On the first floor there were only two bedrooms and there was not even a ceiling between the first floor bedrooms and what would have been attic space. There was no bathroom or shower, just mess everywhere. Mum must have had her hands full trying to sort out the house to prepare for the arrival of her first baby.

Mum grew up having everything spotless and clean. Her mother drove her like a slave to clean the house till no dust was to be seen. Her own mum washed herself until she had sores and eczema on parts of her body. Mum had been taught that almost everything was dirty. For Mum to leave a city and come to a farm brought huge cultural clashes. When Granny brought the sheep into the kitchen to shear the wool and the sheep manure piled up on the kitchen floor—this was a most revolting sight for Mum. Granny's bread baking also put Mum off, as she saw black flies flying into the dough, as the bread was baking. Granny's uncleanliness made Mum sick. Granny, of course, had never learned anything about hygiene. She was a farmer and there were more important things to think about than keeping the house clean. Granny had never been taught anything about personal hygiene or how to clean a house, all she had done all her life was farming and tending to animals. Obviously from very early on there were two worlds colliding.

Chapter 3

A BABY'S CRY

On the farms around the villages in Norway the farmers would brew their own beer. The selling of alcohol in Norway was monopolised; still today you are unable to buy liquour in an ordinary supermarket. During recent years they have allowed selling beer in local supermarkets, but only on certain times and never on Sundays.

I remember when it was brewing time in our house. Dad laughed a lot and had fun in the basement. Loads of sugar and yeast were bought, and a very large cast iron casserole pot that could take at least 100 litres of water was filled. I remember being allowed to have some brown candy sugar that he used for brewing. I don't know how long it took for the beer to ferment, but I guess it was a few weeks before it was ready to drink.

When the word got out that Dad had beer, the farmers came from the nearby farms to test his beer; the one who had just brewed always claimed to be the winner of the best beer. All the farmers were, of course, in no doubt that Dad had the best beer, knowing that by impressing Dad with their kind words, he would serve them up more.

It was this drinking tradition that began the misery and pain in my life. As the farmers got more and more drunk they started to compliment Dad on what a beautiful wife he had. Where on earth had he found such a beautiful woman? This caused Dad to get very suspicious and over the moon jealous. I have been told that Dad got it in his head that one particular farmer must have slept with Mum. Dad said he was able to put two and two together because of how Mum behaved during the other pregnancies. On the four previous pregnancies Mum had been very grumpy and difficult, but when she was pregnant with me she was always happy and smiling. Dad used to say to Mum that that was his evidence that he was not my father, that she was glad to carry another man's child.

Because of Dad's suspicions, when the men started to show their fancy for Mum, all hell broke loose. One by one they would leave the party; they didn't want to be involved in any domestic arguing. The fact that they had said she was beautiful caused Dad such jealousy that he blamed her for flirting with them. When Mum was drunk she always defended herself from the accusations and fought back verbally, but she would eventually lose it completely and spit in Dad's face. The verbal fighting would always end up in them both wanting to kill each other—blood and bits of hair flying everywhere.

When Mum first came to the farm, she didn't smoke or drink. As the years went by, she started smoking, without Dad's knowledge. Somewhere along the line she also started drinking. Perhaps the beer brewing was the cause of her introduction to alcohol, I don't know. She may well have thought that it would be better to join them drinking than to sit sober and listen to them talking rubbish. I do know she must have seen enough of what alcohol did in her own home, how her own father beat his wife when he was intoxicated. All I remember Mum saying when we confronted her with her drinking was that she said "I have to drink to relax." Mum's decision to drink would have terrible consequences, though, for her family.

I was told a story by Mum's sister Wilma of the time when I was still a baby, less than a year old. Wilma visited us from the North. She was engaged to be married and she and her fiancé stayed at the farm for a few weeks during the early winter. By now Mum and Dad went out drinking too. I think maybe the neglect of the kids was well established by now. Mum and Dad were out visiting other farmers who had brewed beer, tasting what their beer was like. Of course this tasting and competition of whose beer was best was just an excuse to get free alcohol.

Whilst they were out, late into the night, Wilma said she heard a baby crying for a long time. Finally she decided to get up and see what was wrong. She didn't realise my parents were still out and no one was around to tend to the baby. She got out of her bed in a daze to try to find the baby that had been crying for such a long time. With so many children in the house she didn't know at first where the sound came from. The sounds led her to my parent's bedroom, where they had left me in my cot. When she opened the door she found that a piece of glass had broken off the window and a pile of snow had blown through the window pane.

My little cot was on the right hand side of the window pane and there was a little night table next to my cot. On the table my milk bottle had frozen right through; it was solid ice. As she walked towards my cot she saw in horror that I had kicked off my duvet. I was only dressed in tiny thin pyjamas and my hands

and feet had already turned blue. She later told me that she was
so inexperienced with children because she hadn't had any of her
own that all she did was cuddle me till I stopped crying and then
she tightly wrapped my duvet around me with a blanket on the
top. Wilma has told me so many times since that she regretted she
hadn't taken me into her own room, so she could defrost me with
the warmth of her own body. She said it was a miracle, though,
that she heard me and that I would have frozen to death if she
hadn't come and covered me up.

There must have been real mayhem in our home the following
summer when my auntie Wilma arrived again. Her dad had also
decided to come for a visit; the problem was that he was a total
alcoholic. This visit encouraged Mum and Dad to start drinking
earlier that summer. Mum's dad sometimes looked after me when
they were out working on the farm. He was never sober; he had
to continue to drink to prevent getting a hangover! He was sick
and tired of me wetting my diapers, so he decided to put a stop to
it. So, as a punishment, whenever I wet my diapers and needed
changing, he would run the tap and hold me so that the ice cold,
snow-melted water would flush down the lower part of my body.
I was told in later years that I screamed, and while I screamed,
he would laugh at his method to stop me wetting my diapers. He
would say, "This will teach the child to keep her diapers dry."
Naturally, I continued to wet my diapers. I also continued to wet
my bed, long after I had stopped using diapers. I very often had a
lot of pain while urinating and everything seemed to burn when
I did. I think I was about the age of eight when I finally stopped
and my bed was dry.

Chapter 4

WHORE CHILD

Excruciating pain went through my whole body, as shouts of "bloody f ***ing whore child" filled the room. I didn't know if I was sleeping or awake, as I suddenly flew across the room, my head hurting so much. My Dad had hauled me out of my sleep, grabbed my head, and dragged me by the hair and out of my bed in the middle of the night. A big crash filled the room as I hit the wall hard on the other side. It was easy to make me fly so far across to the other side because I was a very tiny three year old, and I fell just like a sack of potatoes. I ended up in a foetal position with my arms trying to protect my head and face.

I must have passed out; everything went black, and then suddenly I woke up with pain in my back and head, where my Dad had continued to hit me while he shouted, "This bloody whore child, get her f***ing out of here." All I could do was scream in sheer horror at being awakened in this way. I must have been in total shock. I didn't know if I was in a dream or if it was indeed real. I cried hysterically, "Help me, help me!" All I could see out of the corner of my eye was Mum, but she could hardly stand up because she was so drunk. "Help me, Mum," I screamed, while I flew across the room again like a rag doll. Dad threw me again and I don't remember what happened after that.

It wasn't until years later as an adult, when my siblings were together for a dinner party that I learned the truth about this "dream." They all got a little tipsy and whenever they got tipsy they talked about things from the past. They were talking about some events of our childhood and suddenly they started to talk about that particular time. "Do you all remember Dad's rage when he stormed into the bedroom where Laila slept and dragged her out of her sleep and threw her across the room?" I said to them, "How do you know about that? That was a dream I had, a nightmare, and I haven't told anybody". They all started laughing hysterically and told me how silly I was.

*****

There was never much food around and definitely not before dinner. Mum always had a thing about dinner—she had to have it. I never saw her eating anything before dinner herself; no surprise she was so moody when she went without food, because she worked so hard. She cooked every day. Dinner was the only meal she demanded we all had to attend. At dinner time we all sat around a table and ate together. No other meal was a must. I guess it was the dinner that kept me from starving to death, although during dinner Dad always watched us with hawk eyes, controlling how much we were allowed to eat. I guess there wasn't much food, so we could not take what we wanted and it was not enough to go around. We were never allowed more than two potatoes and not more than two meatballs each. If it was fish it was only one thin slice and two potatoes. I never dared to eat till

I was full in case I was told off for eating too much. I remember I was always starving when I visited friends in my teens.

The only vegetables we had were carrots, sometimes cabbage. I never saw tomatoes, cucumbers or any other greens in my childhood. I didn't even know what they were. The only fruit we ate was in the autumn when the local farmers who grew it would drive around and sell a big shopping bag full for 10. kroner (1 pound). They sold pears, apples and if we were lucky red plums. Sometimes they sold bags of apples and pears that would not be ripe until Christmas. They had to be kept dark and cold in the basement until they were ready to eat.

*****

The first signs we had that my parents had started one of their drinking bouts was when there was no dinner in the house. Mum always used to cook dinner and when there was no smell of dinner in the house, I knew then that trouble was coming. I also knew I would go hungry and not for just a day or two. I was scared all the time when they were drinking but there was nowhere to go. It was impossible to try to hide from them, because our house was high up in the mountains, and there was quite a distance between each farm. My fear was intensified because the house was very dark and spooky; I always had the feeling something was following me as I walked around the house. It was as if evil were all around me. I was terrified of the dark as a child, the tall mountains dominating the terrain. It was very scary.

The normal pattern that indicated trouble was coming was when I saw Mum go in and out of the living room many times during a short period of time. Each time she returned, her appearance changed. Then Dad got suspicious and started to ask questions as to why she was leaving the room so often. He soon found out she had gin! Then he started to disappear also, and I saw them both get more and more inebriated until finally their beers, gin, and homemade spirits were placed on the table. It was always the same story during each of their drinking binges. They were laughing and having fun in the beginning, and then Dad brought out the accordion and started to play and sing. Then the more drunk Mum got, the more she started to complain about the "hell" of a place she was trapped in, that she was tired of being a slave, and that Dad and stolen her youth.

Dad was very jealous and he knew that Mum had had one boyfriend before she met him. When Dad was drunk he always interrogated Mum about that boyfriend, even though she had only been 15 or 16 years old. Soon they argued about everything and they flew in each other's faces. For as long as I can remember, every time my parents drank, I saw Dad hit Mum. He beat her up all over and in the face till her lips burst and her eyes were blue. She fought him back by biting him and scratching his face with her nails till blood ran down his cheeks. It was always a real wrestling match. I remember in my early years trying to get in between them to separate them. I soon learned that was not a good idea, as I was caught getting hit myself.

Mum always ended up saying that she would kill herself. We found her a few times not responding at all and Dad calling for the ambulance. Often she said she wanted to hang herself in the barn, and then she felt everyone would be happier when she was dead. Maybe that is why I was always afraid to go into the barn, in case I saw Mum dead, hanging from a rope. When, later on she started to see a psychiatrist, she often said she would take an overdose of tablets and kill herself that way. When they were drinking I was in constant fear that I would find Mum dead somewhere.

I felt I had a solution in which I could help Mum! When I saw she poured her gin, I was inspired to put my plan into practice. I remember her glass was full of gin, almost to the top. She then topped it up with a tiny drop of water and drank it all in one go. I knew that after a few of those, my mission could begin. When she got up to go to the toilet, I saw she could hardly walk. I had to act fast by grabbing her by the hand and guiding her upstairs. I put her into my tiny cot; she was hardly able to stand. I safely guided my half-conscious mother, till she almost fell like a bundle into my cot. There she would fall asleep like a round ball with her knees almost touching her chin.

I spent a long time trying to drag my duvet over my mother, trying to cover her so that she could have a safe place to sleep. I had to hide her from Dad. If I didn't act quickly enough he would soon find her and hell would break loose. As a tiny girl I was unable to understand that no matter how much I tried to cover Mum with my little duvet, it was obvious that she was sleeping in my bed, as a big heap could be seen under my duvet! The worst thing about it was that my cot was located in my parents' bedroom, so when Dad walked in, he saw Mum immediately. I could not think of any other place I could hide her, but in my tiny cot. Dad always found Mum and my mission to protect her didn't succeed. I felt then that it was my fault and I thought I was a very bad kid. I didn't understand at the time that I was not responsible for my Mum's safety and there was no way for me to protect her from Dad.

Chapter 5

THE TYRANNY OF TED

It was natural for Mum to let my siblings look after me, as she had lots of chores to do on the farm. My siblings were given the responsibility to take me out in the pushchair when I was old enough to sit in it. They went high and low, sometimes far away from the farm. They found it such fun to have a living doll to play with.

In the west of Norway there are many rivers and big waterfalls. I have been told that one day they strayed off with me in the pushchair. We were about to cross a river when one of the wheels got stuck and the pushchair jumped. I flew out through the air and splashed down into the waterfall. My siblings and a few kids from the neighbour's farm were also there, and they almost laughed themselves to death as they saw this tiny child spinning round and round in the river with her hair stuck out at all angles. I spun in the waters like I was in a washing machine. Then Sally suddenly thought to herself, this is maybe not a good idea. Why don't we help Laila? So, at the age of seven, she saved my life from drowning, by pulling me up from the river.

The very first memory I have of Ted was when I was about

14 months old. It was a day when Mum went for a walk with all the kids. It turned out to be a three mile round trip. Eventually, when Mum turned around to walk back home, Ted said he was tired and he started to make a fuss about wanting to sit in my pushchair. He managed to get his own way and as Mum squashed Ted in behind me, he immediately started to push me towards the very thin, unpadded metal pole that was in front of the pushchair. I remember the pain in my belly as he pushed me with his feet for the next 1.5 miles on the way home. Mum did nothing to stop him from trying to kick me out of the pushchair.

There were not many pictures taken of me as a kid, but I do remember once, when Mum decided to take a picture of me and Ted. I was around three years old at the time. She told us we had to hold hands. Ted always said, "I hate her, I hate her, I don't want to touch her, she is a witch." But I wanted my picture taken too, as had all my siblings. I knew that I had to act fast and I also knew the risk I was taking by what I was about to do. But, to get my picture taken, I thought it was worth it.

Mum said, "I won't take your picture unless you hold hands", so I just put my hand in Ted's arm as quickly as I could and smiled on Mum's command, and then Mum snapped the picture. As soon as she had taken the picture, Ted started to beat me up. He grabbed me by my hair and pulled a big handful out. He then went for my face and his nails forced themselves into my face until blood ran down my cheeks. Then he hit me to the floor, and as I was unable to move, he now had an advantage, because he was able to put more force into kicking me. It was as if he knew that I would suffer more pain this way whilst I lay on the floor. I had been through this so many times before and I knew what was coming.

I screamed to Mum for help, but she had long sat down in her chair with a cigarette, was busy reading her weekly magazine, and didn't pay any attention to me crying for help. The pain was excruciating, especially in my stomach this time, because this was where he decided to kick the most. He never wanted to stop. The more I cried the more he kicked, and when I thought he had stopped, he started again. It was as if Ted was driven. When he started to hit me, he just couldn't stop.

Every time Ted hit me, it was as if he decided to allow the "devil" to control him—that is how I saw it.   I always cried for help to Mum. I never gave up hope that she would help me. I always thought she would see Ted for what a tyrant he was. But Mum resigned herself to everything, especially to me crying. I often thought that if I had been born a boy, how different my life might have been. Mum had three girls before she had a boy. Did having a boy make her so happy that when she became pregnant again, she thought she might have another boy? Was I such a big disappointment to her, being a girl?

Crying to Mum for help, when she was just a couple of feet away from where Ted was beating me, was such a dilemma for me. I had all the pain from the beating, but there was another pain inside of me that is hard to explain. It was like a knife hitting the centre of my guts. I experienced an unbelievable fear, seeing my rescuer so near yet not doing anything. It was always as if I was living a nightmare, where rescue was so near, but still so far away. My cries were never heard. I always had to ride the wave out, taking the beatings, whilst always, out of the corner of my eye, I could see Mum just sitting there reading her magazines.

Sometimes Ted and I would play outside with little cars; we played normally like siblings are supposed to. We made roads and little mud houses and used moss for the rooftops on the little houses we made, and everything was okay. When my roads were finished, Ted suddenly had that look in his eyes and I knew his playing was over. His second amusement started—"time to destroy hers"! There were very few days in my childhood when Ted left me alone whilst we were playing. He always destroyed the things I had made and made any excuse to beat me up. This was no ordinary sibling conflict. Ted used tremendous violence. My only defence was my mouth. When he started to destroy the things I had built and demolish my roads, I called him the devil. This stimulated his rage every time and he snapped. I don't know why I had to do that, knowing he would get worse, but I had to say it. There was no other way I could defend myself and exercise my defence

Chapter 6

THE SUMMER SEASON

The farmers in the West of Norway have to harvest their crops as soon as the season begins, as the summers there are very short. We knew summer had come the moment we woke up, and there was that familiar smell of diesel! It was Dad's tractor and he was out in the fields cutting the grass. There was no way anyone could escape, all hands were needed. I was given a tiny rake for a Christmas present one year and I had to use even that, to help rake the grass into piles, ready for the tractor to take into the silos. Dad had a very old tractor and when he filled it with a load of wet grass onto the back, the tractor could not always get the backload into locking position to drive the silage away. Then Mum and my siblings had to help lift the heavy backload into the lock position. Once whilst Dad sat on the tractor, he suddenly shouted at me and told me to throw my rake down and come and help with the lifting, I was around four years old and I thought I didn't have the strength to give any help to such a heavy load, but I was strictly ordered to help.

Ted had been given a sit-on plastic tractor the previous Christmas. When Dad drove to the barn with the silage, everyone had to continue to rake the fields. I saw Ted's tractor parked down by the brook. I so much wanted to have a ride on it! So I ran down to the little brook by the field where he had left it. I knew Ted had said he would kill me if I so much as touched it, but I could not resist the thought of riding the plastic tractor, and I thought to myself that I could drive away from him in this if he comes after me. I imagined the tractor would probably go very fast. I jumped on, but I could not reach the pedals!

The tractor started to roll down towards the brook. I had never been on anything like this before. I was unable to steer it and I plunged straight into the brook where I went under the water. It was so muddy that I could not see a thing. It felt like an eternity before I reached the surface. I was not able to swim so I cried out, and who else was on the bank but Ted!

Ted screamed in rage, "My tractor, my tractor, it's wet! I'll kill you! I'll kill you!"

I reached up with my hand hoping to be rescued before I went under the water again. As I managed to get my head above the water, he kicked me back in. Suddenly, I felt as if my right arm was being pulled out of joint. Mum appeared and dragged me out of the water by one arm. As soon as I was out of the water, she just dropped me on the bank and walked off. She went back to work, raking the fields. No comfort or wiping snot and tears, no making sure I was okay, she just walked off and left me to the mercy of Ted.

For a moment I thought I was safe, having been rescued from the waters. I lay on the bank, exhausted from lack of air and a pain in my chest after swallowing so much water. Finally, I coughed up some of the water that was stuck in my throat. All I wanted to do was sleep.

Suddenly, though, I heard the screaming voice of Ted; he came towards me in a furious rage, after wiping the water off his tractor. He had one of his violent fits again and I knew, this time, I had touched something that was his, and I knew he would beat me to death if he caught me. I didn't die in the brook, but I knew for sure that I would not live through this. He beat me until I was not able to make another sound, or cry for Mum's help.

*****

Finally, after weeks of hard work it was all finished, the grass was in the silos and the dry hay was in the barn. We always celebrated the end of the harvest season by cooking a special traditional type of porridge, made from sour cream and plain flour. I thought that it was the best porridge in the whole world, all the sweat and work was worth one portion of that. It was lovely, with sugar and cinnamon sprinkled on the top, finished off with melted butter, and at this special event we were served red squash. We invariably had to drink water with everything, so red squash was a real treat.

The end of the harvest season, though, brought a new season of drinking. Each summer Mum would want to go up North, where she came from, to visit her Mum and her sister. Dad never wanted to go so far and always tried to find excuses to delay the time for them to go. The trip took two days. It was a 600 mile long journey. In those days the roads were very bad, and it seemed to take forever. Today in Norway the maximum speed is still only 50 miles per hour. Only in a few places on special motorways are you allowed to drive 65 miles per hour.

During the summer of 1969 when I was just three years old,

I can clearly remember Dad having a red Opel car. In the front there was one long single seat, rather than two separate seats. I felt so proud to sit between the driver and the passenger and I felt so lucky to sit above everyone else and to be able to see clearly out of the car. When we went on holidays that year it was wonderful; I felt like a princess! I had a whole front seat to myself, no hassle and far away from Ted. I don't remember anything else of the holiday that year, only that I was able to sit there and feel so special. But that would change dramatically in just a few years.

The summer of 1972 was very different. I was about six years old. Mum and Dad had started to drink right after the harvest was finished. Mum had suddenly decided that she had waited long enough for Dad to take us on holiday to visit her family. Dad continued to make excuses, saying there was still too much to be done on the farm. Further drinking and continued arguments led to Mum screaming at Dad saying she wanted to make the trip. Finally, he agreed in a furious rage, shouting "I'll give you your f***ing holiday! Let's go now! Let's go on your f***ing holiday!" He then threw all the clean clothes Mum had prepared out through the back door into the dirty farmyard. They had just bought a new white Opel and this one had two separate seats at the front, not one long one like the old car had. My new place in the car from now on was on the floor by my Mum's feet. I used to lie on a rug and have a blanket over me. I had to hide when we went on ferry crossings because Mum didn't want to pay my fare. I never saw anything on the long journeys after that; I was stuck on the floor. At least I was away from Ted and he was unable to get at me. I believe Mum put me there, so that she could have some quiet in the car on such a long journey.

Mary and Sally refused to come on holiday that year. Mary ran off and hid in the manure basement on the neighbouring farm. Sally was unable to escape Dad and he grabbed her outside the house in our garden. Some redcurrant bushes were planted there and the garden gently sloped down towards the road. I was stunned as I saw Dad fight with Sally till they fell over, she tried to get loose of his grip, then they rolled down the slope of our garden. He was wrestling with his 12 year old daughter! Mum had just sewn us all new summer clothes and she spent ages getting them ready for the holiday. I saw Dad tear her clothes off into pieces as he fought with her. She finally escaped Dad's grip and ran off.

A moment later Dad rushed into the house. As I stood in the yard I suddenly saw loads of clothes being thrown out into the dirt towards the car again. He came back out and threw the rest of the clothes into the car and said to Mum to get the hell into the car. "You wanted your f***ing holiday, and you will get your f***ing holiday." Dad threw me into the car; Angela and Ted were already waiting to go, and then we drove off. I don't know how many hours we drove, but he was very drunk.

In Norway in July the nights are normally very light. It doesn't get dark until very late and then just for a few hours, and it's not too dark even then. I do remember though it was quite dark now and Mum repeatedly told Dad to stop the car but he didn't care. She then grabbed the car keys out of the car as he was driving it. This caused the wheel to go into lock and he was unable to steer the car and we went straight off the road into a ditch.

I thought this was really exciting. There was trouble and I didn't cause it! Suddenly another car stopped and a tall man and his wife started talking to Mum and Dad. They asked Mum and

Dad if they had been drinking. Dad said that it was an accident. He explained Mum had pulled the keys out of the car for fun. He went on to say that in the old red Opel they used to have, they could do it for fun to scare people, because you were still able to drive the car even if someone pulled out the keys during driving. But in this new car, it was impossible to remove the keys without the steering wheel locking. Somehow they managed to convince the people of this lie.

I decided this was a good opportunity to start to cry. I thought the situation deserved a tear or two, so as I began to cry, this tall man lifted me up and comforted me. It was a strange feeling being lifted up, sitting on his arm. I thought he must be the strongest man in the whole wide world to be able to lift me, now that I was such a big girl. Six years old and I couldn't remember what it felt like to be lifted up and to be sat on someone's arm before. I remember studying every detail of his profile, his ears, nose and the fact that he had not shaved. I was able to look at his hair that was combed back in an Elvis style. I didn't know who Elvis was then, but that was the style of his blonde hair.

I soon stopped crying. This new feeling of safety had a quickly calming effect on me. This strong man stroked my cheeks and he finally gently put me back on the ground that was so far down. I remember thinking I would love to sit on this man's arm forever and never leave him. Reluctantly, I walked towards the car that was being pulled up from the ditch. I so much wanted to be with the man who had lifted me up and held me. The last thing I wanted was to go back to my parents! I felt so afraid and alone with them. The trip continued and I don't remember much more than lying on the floor by Mum's feet.

Chapter 7

ON HOLIDAY

We arrived at Nan's house in the North after a two day long journey. Nan lived in the downstairs part of the house and my auntie Wilma lived upstairs. The normal procedure on all our holidays was that Mum and Dad found the nearest liquor store and got their well deserved drinks.

Nan was always so glad to see us, but soon she would start to complain about how thin I was, and the dark blue circles under my eyes. She was obsessed with my cough. "Stop it, stop it" she would say. "Why don't you cough properly and get it all out in one go." Nan didn't realise that I was sleeping in my parents' bedroom and they were smoking before they went to bed and also in the middle of the night. My parents' cigarettes never left their mouths; I was constantly exposed to smoke. I had constant throat infections and very often pain in my ears; coughing was something that I could not stop even if I wanted to.

After Mum and Dad's obligatory first stop at Nan's, they went to see Mum's dad. He lived in a tiny cabin with no electricity. There was a horrible smell of soot there and I remember it was very dirty. There were three wooden steps up to his cabin and they were covered with beer bottle tops, which he had nailed down one by one until the stairs were covered. I have never seen so many beer bottle tops in my whole life.

Mum's dad started to command us to give messages to Nan. "Tell your f***ing Nan from me, that she is a bloody witch and she is mad, she is a whore of whores. Tell that bloody f***ing witch that I hope she drops dead, she is a crazy bitch and she is the daughter of satan". He was shouting and screaming one horrible word after another and he made me think he was angry with me! When he had finished his tirade of hate for Nan, he would start to laugh and joke with Mum and Dad.

Of course the party was now on!

Angela, Ted and I were left to care for ourselves. Many hours went by just waiting outside his cabin; we went in to ask for food. Mum's dad said, "Here is some money for ice-cream; this will keep the kids away for a long time." He explained where the kiosk was, and we realised it was going to be a long walk. I thought all my birthdays had come at once and off we went. Maybe Mum's dad wasn't so bad after all, I thought to myself. Several hours went by and we had our well deserved ice cream, which was the only food I remembered eating that day.

When we went back home to Nan, she started to question us about her ex-husband. I didn't dare to say all those things he told me to tell her. Now it was her turn to give us "messages" to give to him. "Tell that f***ing bastard, that devil of a man, I hope he falls and breaks his neck. He is from hell and is the son of satan. There aren't any people more evil than him. He is the biggest jerk on earth; he could just go and shoot himself. I hope someone will poison him and he has a very slow and painful death." At such a young age I was unable to comprehend the rage my grandparents felt for each other. But year after year I just got used to their shouting and the messages they wanted to send to each other through me.

At Nan's place Mum and Dad's drinking continued. Angela and Ted had some money and they decided to go to town and buy some sweets. I wanted to go too so I followed them. It was approximately a two mile walk to town. Nan's house is located high up in the hills so it was not too hard to keep up with them. When we arrived in town, Angela and Ted chose what chocolate they wanted. I said to them, "Where is my chocolate? I want one too." They just laughed and said "You get your own money and buy your own chocolate."

I turned around to go back to Nan's and as I ran through the streets I thought would lead to her house, I found myself lost. I found my way back to the kiosk where my siblings had bought their chocolate. They had long gone and I started to walk through the streets of the town. It was impossible for me to find my way back home, no matter how I searched. At the age of six, I had not yet learned to pay any attention to the surroundings where we walked, I remember just taking one step at a time.

Several hours went by and I was lost in town. I decided this was a situation that deserved a good cry. I covered my face with my hands and started crying. It didn't take long before a taxi driver stopped his car and asked if I was lost. I explained the situation and the taxi driver told me to jump in and he would help me find my location. He kept asking me what Nan's name was and what her address was. I said her name is Nan and she lives in a white house up a hill. After a while the taxi driver was about to give up. Then suddenly I saw Mum and Wilma walking down the street. I shouted to the taxi driver, "There is Mum, there is Mum!" Although I was a bit scared of being lost, it was a wonderful feeling to find it had caused such a fuss. It had even brought Mum out to look for me!

Every summer we visited Nan for just two weeks. Afterwards, we faced the long journey back home, where I had to lay on the floor in the car by Mum's feet all the way. But I loved coming home because I had missed Granny and Granddad

Chapter 8

GRANDDAD

There was always great competition to please Grandma and Granddad. One of the regular things Granny would ask us kids to do was to bring them the newspaper. With three generations living in the same household we only had one newspaper. When the postman came it was always such a thrill to run and get it, so that Granddad could have it first.

I always remember Granddad being very old. He was born the 11th June 1894. He was very wrinkly and his hands and head were always shaking. His fingers were curled in a strange way and he could not straighten them. He had very little hair on the top of his head and what was left was grey. He had a short trimmed moustache and he still had some of his own teeth. When he went to bed, he laid in his bed reading his cowboy books, holding them up very close to his face, reading with a tiny light from the night lamp on the wall behind him. He had lost one of his eyes after an accident when a small stone was trapped in his eye. For years the trapped stone caused an infection that led the doctors to remove his eye. So every night he took out his glass eye and put it in a cup before he went to sleep.

Some times I would ask Granny if I could please sleep in her bed. I called her my stove, because she was always warm and I was like an ice cube and I felt she would defrost me. I loved to hear Granddad's stories from the real old days. He told us about the wolves that came around the houses then, and how they had to be careful when they went to feed the animals to make sure they shut the barn door, because wolves would surround the barn in large packs and howl for the animals inside. He told me stories about how the bears attacked the cattle while they were in the mountains during the summer and how they would go out in big hunting teams to hunt the bears down. I was so fascinated with everything Granddad had seen and experienced, even surviving two world wars, and I always wanted to hear the stories again and again. Granddad was my brave hero and he had lived for so long I thought he would live forever!

Each morning that I woke up with Granny and Granddad, one of them would always bring coffee in bed. Granny was tired in the mornings, so it was more often Granddad brought the coffee to help wake her up. Sometimes Granddad could not find either the milk or the coffee, and then Granny would have to jump out of bed, with tiny half asleep eyes, run into the kitchen, and help Granddad find everything. He always put two biscuits on the saucer and made instant coffee with loads of milk. I loved the biscuits and enjoyed the coffee too.

Then Granddad brought in bread crumbs that he had crushed the day before to feed the little birds. He would call the birds, after he put the food on their tray, and soon the little birds came flying from everywhere to get their food. Granddad said he felt he had to look after the little birds, and he said, "Laila, you will always be my little bird." So when Granddad talked to me, he often said, "You come here, my little bird!" When Granddad became sick with cancer, he asked me if I would continue to feed the birds when he was not able to. I promised him to do my best, and for years after his death I gave his birds the food.

I often sat in Granny's kitchen; I liked to draw there. Granddad used to teach me how to draw. With his shaky hands, he would show me how to draw a horse. It took ages for him to get it right. It almost lulled me to sleep seeing his old hand trying to draw a horse whilst chewing his tobacco, the brown saliva running down the deep wrinkles on each side of his mouth, taking short breaks to spit in the sink as his mouth got too full. I so much loved drawing at my Granddad's kitchen table, with him there to help me get my drawings right.

One day, Dad suddenly came storming through the door, drunk as a skunk, in raging anger. He screamed, "Where in the hell is my f***ing newspaper, where in the hell is the f***ing newspaper?" Granny was washing the dishes. She turned around when she saw her son run towards her husband. It all happened so quickly that there was no time for her to interfere. Granddad stood by the stove with the newspaper in his hand and Dad ran towards his father and hit him with full force across his head. The next thing I saw was Granddad on the floor, the newspaper flying out of his hands. I ran to try to rescue Granddad, but I was too late. Granny was shouting "Stop!", but she was too late too. Dad grabbed the newspaper that had landed on the floor and stormed out of the room, just as quickly as he had arrived, slamming the door behind him, curse words ringing through the house. Granny managed to get Granddad back up on his feet and they rang Sara, their daughter. She came and took Granddad to the doctor. For a long time Granddad had to wear a neck brace; Dad had broken his collarbone!

Granny knew it was getting too dangerous to stay for long periods at the farm after this episode, especially during the times when Mum and Dad were drinking. She and Granddad decided to stay away for longer periods of time. But this was the house where my Granddad was born! He was homesick, so they came home just now and again. In 1973 their daughter Sara had moved into her new house 30 miles away, and Granny and Granddad started to stay there.

The absence of Granny and Granddad brought a lot more hardship for me. There was no one I could run to when Ted was after me, nowhere I felt safe at all. The only refuge I had left now was my dog Tally. I loved her from the moment she came to the farm. The first greeting Tally gave me was when she ran over and jumped up on me. I fell over and she licked me all over. She was one year old when we had her and I was just six. She became my best friend, in fact my only friend.

Tally had a mat under the kitchen table, she and the cat used to sleep there together. I used to be so cold all the time. I wore hand-me-down tights that were far too big; they were at least six inches too long. My feet were always a problem to me in that old, cold house. But I figured out a way to help myself when it got too cold. I used to crawl under the kitchen table and cuddle up to Tally and my cat. I remember snuggling up tightly to Tally's belly and grabbing the cat to get heat from them. I often fell asleep with the two lovely warm animals. I started to daydream about one day getting married and leaving this place. My plan was to marry a tall man with big muscles that could box Ted in the stomach when he came after me, and also knock out my Dad's teeth when he became cruel.

There were no words of comfort that Tally could give me: I

often wished she could be my very own wolf who would put an end to Ted's tyranny. But Tally would wag her tail at whoever came to the farm. With Tally's wonderful happy nature and her warm body, I felt she was essential for my survival after Granny left. At least she was someone I could talk to and cry with and Tally was the one I felt really listened to me. When things got really bad, Tally was the only one I could run to and pour out my grief.

One day I said to Mum, "I want to go and visit Granny." I was about six or seven years old and not old enough to start school yet. I wanted to go and visit her for a week. In Norway in the 70's you had to be seven before you could start school so Mum said that I was not allowed to go. But I didn't care, I had never been taught boundaries. I wanted to see Granny and that settled it for me. I found a shopping bag, packed a change of clothes and stood by the road waiting for a car. I had seen how Mary and Sally managed to stop the cars by holding out their right thumb. After a long time I got lucky and I was so happy to be on my way to see Granny. After one week it was time for me to go home, and Granny gave me enough money to take the bus. But there where no way I was going to spend the money on a bus! I wanted to save it. So I ran a shortcut down to another road and decided to return home the same way I had arrived!

When I came home, everything was normal; I was not told off or punished. I wasn't asked any questions about where I had been or what I had been doing because I had told Mum that I wanted to see Granny. But I do guess that Granny may have called Mum to say that I had arrived. There were no boundaries given, though. If Mum said no to something, we just did it anyway, and there were never any consequences of just doing what we wanted.

Chapter 9

THE SCARY GAME

Auntie Sara and her son Ken sometimes came to visit the farm. This time Granny and Granddad were home for a few weeks too. They made sure to come when they knew my parents weren't drinking. We used to play for hours outside in the deep snow, digging big tunnels and building snow huts under the snow. We also climbed onto the roof of the barn and glided on our backsides down the roof. It sent us in a free fall of 12 feet before we hit a big pile of snow beneath. Only our heads were left above ground after the big fall. It was very difficult to crawl out after being stuck so firmly in the snow. All this activity made us very tired after playing. So after Ken, Ted and I had finished playing outside for hours it was time to go inside. It was a relief to have played outside for such a long time without Ted getting at me. Then I suddenly saw Ted's eyes change!

This change I always recognised as the "devil" eyes. We were on our way in and I was not too far away from the door when I asked Ken to bring me my sleigh. Ted suddenly shouted, "Don't bring it to her!" I was so tired I begged Ken to please bring me my sleigh. Ted shouted, "If you bring her the sleigh, I will f***ing kill her, I'll kill her." But Ken felt sorry for me, having to walk all the way back to the barn to get my sleigh, so he picked it up to bring it to me. As Ken grabbed my sleigh, Ted ran towards me, and I knew I had to make a quick move, but my wellies suddenly got stuck in the snow and I could not get loose for a moment.

This delayed me long enough for Ted to dive towards me, grabbing my head and plunging it into the snow. As he did, he dug the snow from beneath my head and kept filling my mouth with snow. This was no ordinary plunging in the snow; this was a mission to kill! Ted's anger was such that the angrier he got, the more he "lost" it. It was as if he suffered blackouts; he could not stop once he began, and he seemed to be driven into a trance, enjoying my pain.

I don't know how long I was without air, but there was no way I could resist his heavy weight on top of my back, holding my head in a solid lock under the snow. I gave up trying to breathe and resigned myself not to wake up. Suddenly, I felt his weight lift and he got off me and walked inside the house. He probably thought he had succeeded in his mission to kill me, when he felt there was no more resistance from me.

Once I finally managed to spit all the snow out of my mouth and blow the snow out of my nose, I used the little strength I had left to pick myself up and to walk inside. I cried as I went straight to my Granny's living room and she asked me what was wrong. I told her what had happened and she said I'd better lie down on her sofa and take a rest. While I lay there it was such a relief, knowing that Granny was home, for I knew my brother could not get at me while she was near. I was lying there thinking, I wish my Granny could stay forever and she didn't have to go away again. I dreamt of being her only girl and that we would be together forever. But Granny came and went again and I was left in my own care.

*****

I can't remember any routine at bedtime. I was never told when to have supper, to wash or to brush my teeth. We were one of the first farms in the area to have a TV. So a typical night, when there was no drinking of alcohol, was when Mum and Dad watched whatever was on the TV. We had a very small living room where the TV was located and I can remember always having to lie on the floor at the end of an evening, trying to get underneath the thick blanket of smoke.

Every Friday night the American show "Gunsmoke" was shown on TV. I loved to see that western series. By the end of the show, I used to pretend that I had fallen asleep on the floor, so that Mum would pick me up and put me in my bed. I found out this was the only way I could get picked up and feel like I was a kid.

On the farm next to ours, lived four boys and two girls. They were the same age as my siblings and they all went everywhere together. I was always told to "bugger off" and leave them alone. But each time I sneaked after them to see what they where doing. In our barn the dry soft hay reached at least eight feet high. The hay was not stored in bundles or piles like they are these days. The hay was simply shovelled high up to cover half the barn upstairs. Downstairs we had sheep and some hens. Mum had refused to continue to have cows and goats when they took over the farm some years earlier. She only wanted to have sheep so that she was able to go on holiday to visit her Mum, whilst the sheep could be left in the wilds for the summer season.

My siblings had made little huts and also a little shop high up in the barn. They had collected all sorts of empty bags and filled them with hay seeds, baking powder, sugar bags, tins of meatballs, coffee bags and all sorts of stuff. I also followed them around while they were playing. We played like acrobats high up, on the planks and poles that went across the ceiling of the barn. We were never afraid to fall down; it never occurred to us that it might be dangerous.

They also built long deep tunnels in the hay, and dug tunnels all the way down to the floor, where they dug a cave and used it like a hut. They had all started to smoke by now and while we were down inside the hay, where they thought they were safe from being seen by Dad, one of the kids lit up a cigarette. I thought that smoking was very exciting, but then suddenly they wised up and said we needed to put out the cigarette because the hay might catch fire.

In the spring all the farmers have a lot of work to do. Everyone prepares to get ready for the harvest—clearing rubbish from the barn, fixing broken vessels, building things that need to be built, brushing and cleaning out the empty silos for new grass and so on. Our barn had two silos--each one was 30 feet deep. One of the silos had a ceiling, but the other was only partly covered. Knowing the kids played high and low in the barn, Dad began to complete the ceiling on that silo. I was running around high up on the planks and poles in our barn and wanted to check out what Dad was doing.

Without knowing that his work had not finished, I ran across the newly built ceiling to pass right in front of Dad. He was down on all fours, nailing down the planks, and there was a big hole right in front of him that he was about to cover. I didn't see the hole and as I ran across it I fell straight down. In a split second and with pure reflex reaction my Dad barely managed to grab the wrist of my right hand as I was on my way down. If he had been a microsecond later he would have missed my hand and I would have fallen 30 feet down onto solid concrete to a sure death below. He shouted, "Get the hell away from here" as he threw me across the top of the silo, and I landed in the soft hay like a bundle several feet down, safe and sound.

I was more terrified over the flight down to the hay, than I had been falling into the silo. I did not know that I had been in great danger. I started to cry because I was so scared over the fall and everything happening so fast, but there was never any kind of comfort given, or questions like "Are you okay?" I sat there, trying to figure out what had just happened. I didn't realise at that time or for quite a few minutes after, that Dad had saved my life. But when I finally understood, I thought, maybe he doesn't hate me after all!

One condition my sister Angela laid down if I was to go with her, was for me to take the leftover cigarettes from my parents, so that she could roll her own. When I saw that everyone smoked I thought to myself, I had better start doing this too. I thought I would be grown up and get big if I smoked. So at the age of seven, I started to smoke. I lit up the first cigarette of my own and inhaled it. I didn't like it at all, I think because I was exposed to so much smoke during the daytime and also during the night. I always struggled with a bad cough that has never left me. But because I was so used to inhaling Mum and Dad's smoke, I didn't cough when I inhaled the first one of my own. I felt very grown up with a cigarette in my mouth, and I was so proud when I learned how to puff smoke rings out of my mouth. It was also so cool to blow the smoke out my nose; it was funny to play with the smoke.

When Granny and Granddad went to stay at Sara's for long periods of time, Mum demanded that Granny give up one of her two bedrooms to Sally. This was the bedroom in which I had knelt down and prayed to Jesus to rescue me. The room was located in the attic; Mary had already one room up there on one side of the attic and now Sally was going to join her on the other side. They were both teenagers so they needed their own rooms. There was a hallway in between the two bedrooms, and that was where the old rubbish was stored. When my siblings got a bit older they stopped playing in the barn and they would indulge in other things that teenagers often did.

Sometimes in the evening, the kids from the other farm would come over to visit my siblings. They played poker and other card games. They also competed to stay up all night and not go to bed, to see who would last the longest. I was always very tired trying to copy all they did, but I also managed to do their "wake nights" as they called it. I was not allowed to play any card games with them; I just sat there watching them. At least it was entertainment for me to see who would win the games.

I think they were bored of playing poker all the time. So they found other scary games to play. They cut out big pieces of greaseproof paper and drew circles with a pen around a glass. Once they had enough circles for each letter of the alphabet, they wrote the letters on the circles. They took a big sheet of glass and after tightly wrapping a large piece of greaseproof paper around a plank of wood they placed the sheet of glass on the top. The last thing they needed was a glass which they put upside down on the Ouija board. The only other thing they needed was darkness and then the game began. I tried to become invisible in the corner of the room as they started their game.

Everyone sat in a circle around the Ouija board and held their hands above the glass. It was as quiet as the grave. I could barely hear anyone breathing, when the sound of the glass started to move. It was always scary but weirdly exciting when they called on the king of darkness to appear. It was always the word "satan" that came up on the Ouija board. One time, after calling on satan, we all saw a ball of green yellowish light the size of a plum flying back and forth across the tiny bedroom. We all screamed with fright and someone put the light on.

I think that it was after attending the games with my siblings, that I started to feel that evil was following me all the time and that this evil wanted to kill me.

Chapter 10

A NEW ESCAPE, CHRISTMASTIME
AND MY BIRTHDAY

I felt hungry and tired. Mum and Dad had been drinking for several weeks, and I hadn't had enough to eat. I didn't know where Mum and Dad were, but I knew I needed to go to bed. I went upstairs and crawled into my bed. It was not a big bed, just a small cot about three feet long, the same cot I had since I was born. I had no mattress. I slept on blankets and it was very hard and I always ached when I got up. I had wet my cot for a long time and because Mum was drunk all the time, she hadn't changed my bedding.

This caused green and grey hairy mould to grow through my sheets. The hot water bottle had gone cold days ago and there was no source of heat. I tried to curl up away from the worst mouldy parts of my cot, but it was so small that it was inevitable that I came into contact with it.

I was so afraid that Dad would come and pull me out of my sleep and hit me! I didn't know how to relax. As I laid there I felt a sense of despair and loneliness and fear. It was impossible for me to sleep. I was too exhausted from the awful cold and painful hunger.

I don't know how I came up with this idea, but I suddenly found a way to help me relax. I started to knock and shake my head on the hard surface of my cot. I knocked and knocked until I felt giddy, then I would shake my head sideways. I did this repeatedly until I was so exhausted I fell asleep, which always seemed to take ages.

I often woke up in the middle of the night in pain, because I had knocked my head in my sleep and sometimes I would have hit my head on the side plank of my wooden cot. I was always very tense and unable to relax. I experienced such great fear. The only way I felt I had any reprieve was when I caused myself to go giddy. Sometimes I saw stars and the room would really spin around fast. I went into a world of my own like this, and it was all spinning, I felt no one could get to me. This was MY world, and only I was in it. For the rest of my childhood I continued to knock my head on the mattress every night when I went to bed. It became my form of escape.

*****

In Norway it's traditional to celebrate Advent, the four Sundays before Christmas and we light one candle every Sunday in memory of Jesus. In our basement Dad always stored a lot of fire wood. One day Angela and I went down to the basement to find a proper log, one in which we could drill four holes to fit the candles, preparing a nice Advent candle holder, covered with fir needles and drizzled with cotton wool to make it look like snow. Towards Christmastime, Mary, Sally, Angela, Ted and I, would go out to find a Christmas tree in the forest, always on the 23rd of December on what we called Little Christmas Eve. I remember always going onto our neighbour's land to chop down trees. We never failed to find one to fit our living room. Mum and Dad always bought a whole box of 24 bottles of pop for us to enjoy during Christmas and we would choose our favourite flavour to have with our meal. We put our own pop on the table where we were to sit. (The only other time we had pop during the year was on Midsummer Eve. It is celebrated with bonfires all over Norway. Then, Mum bought one litre of pop to share, which meant we had one glass each.)

The Christmas spirit felt good when we came home and decorated the tree. The following day, the 24th, is the day that we celebrate Christmas in Norway. We always begged Mum and Dad not to drink and every year they gave their promise not to drink. The only alcohol they promised to take was one beer with their Christmas meal and that was it. But they were not promise keepers. They both did their normal disappearing act and came back more drunk each time!

At five pm the meal would be ready but by now Mum and Dad were quite tipsy. One of the girls found out where they had hidden their big bucket of beer in the basement. She then told Mum and Dad that she had poured out all the alcohol. She wanted to teach them a lesson to show them they could not hide their drinking from us. This made Dad furious! He said that if the kids had poured out his beer, they would not have any pop for Christmas either! He ran out into the cold hallway where the box of pop was stored, grabbed it and rushed outside to the stone stairs. There he dropped the whole box of glass pop bottles from the first floor down to the freezing ground a few metres below. All the bottles broke except one. We all cried! The pop was meant to last all over Christmas. Having pop was one of the highlights of the year. One of my sisters hadn't chosen a pop for herself. I saw her running down to the freezing ground to try to find a bottle of pop that was not broken, so she could have one too. Among all the broken pieces of glass she suddenly spotted the only bottle that was whole. Dad calmed down when he went down to the basement and found his beer and spirit safely stored where he had left it. But, we had no more pop that Christmas.

A tradition we enjoyed when Granddad and Granny lived at the farm was that we all sang a psalm of thanksgiving before eating our Christmas meal. It only happened one day a year.

One Christmas, Mum suddenly shouted out in rage, "Why on earth should we sing to God only at Christmas? I don't want to do this nonsense anymore. I don't want to be a hypocrite." I felt sad to hear her saying that, because I thought a part of Christmas was singing thanks to God before we ate. There was no more pop and now we were not allowed to sing either. Christmas felt different after we stopped singing the "thank you song".

Once we had eaten our food, the time would arrive to form a circle around the tree and walk around it singing Christmas carols. Every year after quite a few carols, Dad always said that he needed to go to the toilet. He would complain he had eaten too much and that his stomach hurt. I would wait for Dad to leave the room, because I knew it was usually only a few minutes after, that Santa Claus would be knocking at the door and the highlight of the night would arrive. I sometimes felt sorry for Dad, as he always missed Santa's visit. I thought maybe he would not get so angry all the time, if he could only meet Santa!

Anyway, I had one great hug a year and that was from Santa. I sure looked forward to my yearly hug, just as much as my Christmas presents! This Christmas though, Dad did not leave to go to the toilet. I thought that was good, as he would now get to see Santa too! Ted suddenly left the living room. Moments later we heard a knock on the door, but this year it was a much smaller Santa visiting us with a big bag of gifts. I ran forward and threw my arms in the air to hug Santa, but as fast as I approached him the faster Santa pushed me, with such a great force that I fell backwards and banged my head on the hard wooden floor. I thought immediately, this was not Santa! This is the well known devil. There were no more Santa visits again after that year.

That year Mum gave me ten Krone (1 pound) so that I could buy presents for everyone. I spent a long time trying to find something nice for everyone. The shop had nothing on sale cheap enough so I could not buy seven presents for ten Krone.

Finally, I found a bag of ten beautiful shiny conifer baubles, I didn't know that they were Christmas decorations, but the colours were so beautiful. I thought long and hard trying to decide who should have which colour. The one with gold I decided to give to Mary. I was not fussed over the silver one, so I gave that one to Ted, the green one was my favourite colour, so I wanted Sally to have that one, the red one I was sure Angela would like. I opened the sealed bag and took out those I didn't need and went to pay. I later realised that I was stupid leaving three baubles, as the price on the bag was for all of them. Anyway, I thought that I had made a fantastic find, and I was sure that everyone would think this was the best present they would get this year, because they were so shiny, and I loved them!

I waited with excitement for Christmas to come and I boasted to everyone that they would love the present I would give them this year. I was so happy that I didn't think about what presents I was going to get, I was just overwhelmed with excitement over how happy they would all be when they had my present.

When they opened their presents from me, I was waiting to see their faces. I had told them beforehand that I had got something really nice for everyone. When they unwrapped my gift they all laughed themselves silly and held the baubles up and said, "Look at this stupid decoration! Laila is so unintelligent. What an idiot. What on earth does she think we want to use this for, she doesn't know it's a stupid Christmas decoration!" They were right of course, I didn't realise that they were Christmas decorations. I just loved the look of them because they were shiny and thought they would like it too!

Anyway, I was given the most beautiful big baby doll for Christmas, which I still have to this day. I have kept almost all the toys I had as a child. They fit in a small cardboard box that I store in my attic. I had one doll before this one and it was much smaller, and it was made of a very hard type of plastic. Once Ted was in a rage he took my doll and put it between the door and the door frame and smashed the door on my doll's head into irreparable pieces. The arrival of my new doll, the size of a real baby, made up for Dad's rage in breaking all the pop bottles, and the disappointment of the cruel Santa.

After a few hours we finished unwrapping all our gifts. By now Mum and Dad were very drunk. The normal arguing started again and Christmas came and went. I was just happy that I would not wait too long before I had more presents, because just two months after Christmas, would be my birthday.

*****

Every year Mum made loads of cakes for all our birthdays. Angela's was on the 6th and mine on the 7th of February. Mum always served lovely home made hot chocolate too. I felt that everyone threw a big fuss over Angela's birthday but not mine, because we always held a big party on the 6th. I nagged Mum to allow me to open my present on Angela's birthday too. She reminded me in a strict voice that my birthday is on the 7th and that I would have to wait until then to open my present. I didn't feel that it was my birthday on the 6th, because I was not allowed my present. It was always boring on my birthday on the 7th; the party was the day before and it was my sister's party, there was never any fuss over me, all the cakes were cut, no setting up with a nice table with hot chocolate in fancy cups.

On my birthday I woke up and Mum gave me my present. We had cakes and so on, but it wasn't like the day before. I was happy over the present I got, this year a beautiful pushchair for my new doll. I thought I was in heaven and wrapped my doll in a blanket and felt like a proper mum caring for my baby. Ted hated to see me happy and smiling. The next morning before I got up, he had taken a knife and cut the plastic seat on each side of the pushchair my doll was sitting on.

He never got a spanking for anything he did. I was so happy the day before, but now I felt that he had ruined everything. I had this great pushchair for my doll on my birthday and now Ted had destroyed it. I cried and cried without any way of easing my disappointment. When I ran to Mum with my pushchair and showed her, she just glanced up from her magazine, before continuing to read while Ted stood across the room wearing a grinning smile on his face.

Chapter 11

MUM'S RAGE

I ran as fast as I could. Ted was chasing me and wanted to beat me up. I ran around the living room table, then I managed to get out the door into the hallway. There I heard the washing machine running in the bathroom and hoped Mum was there. I burst through the door and Mum stood next to the washing machine with a cigarette in her mouth waiting for the spinner to stop. I grabbed Mum's apron and cried, "Help me! Help me! Ted is after me, help me, Mum!" The feeling of being so near Mum with Ted chasing me, gave me a split second sense of safety, that is until I suddenly felt an excruciating pain across my face.

Mum grabbed me by my hair and dragged me out of the bathroom. She continued hitting me all over my head, particularly across my face and nose. She dragged me through the hallway saying nothing, just hitting me all the time, then up the 12 stairs, across the hall and into the bedroom before she threw me into my cot. Then she stalked out of the room, slamming the door behind her. I sobbed with pain and I was in a kind of shock to think that Mum would beat me up for expecting her to rescue me from Ted! I felt wet all over my face and I tried to wipe it with my hands, but what I thought were tears was blood. It covered my hands. It continued to flow and I thought I would be unable to stop the bleeding.

Moments passed and suddenly there was a pool of blood in my cot. I felt very dizzy as I stepped out of my cot and wobbled across the floor towards the windowsill. The window was already wide open. I slowly leaned forward and hung half my body out through the window. My bleeding nose continued to flow and the blood hit the ground like raindrops falling two floors below me, until it formed a pool.

I lifted my head slightly and saw a beautiful summer day. The fields were covered with thick long grass, with beautiful summer flowers in all colours, the mountains stood tall and strong and each mountaintop was covered with a white cap of snow. I heard the birds singing in the trees around the house. I glanced towards a blackbird sitting on a branch in the tree. Suddenly it lifted its wings and flew off. I thought to myself, why didn't God create me to be a bird, why did he make me a girl? If I had wings I would fly off over the tall mountains and far, far away from here.

In the midst of the beauty all around me, I felt like giving up and just letting my body fall out of the window. I thought that if I did, my neck would break and I wouldn't have to cry anymore. I slowly leaned further forward and my belly was now almost over the edge.

Then out of nowhere I heard one of the girls from the neighbouring farm shouting, "Be careful! Pull yourself in!" She was walking down the road alongside Sally. A slight moment of embarrassment hit me as I pulled myself back into the room. Before I knew it, they had quietly run up the stairs and come into the room without anyone seeing them. They tried to wipe off some of the blood from my face with a towel. Then they took me by my hand and quietly guided me across the floor, out of the house and took me for a walk. They asked me what had happened and I told them. Sally told me not to care and not to worry. I was safe now. I was grateful for their kindness to me, but each time, I experienced the horror of being beaten, I felt more and more empty and the sense of hopelessness got stronger and stronger.

*****

Every year on the 17th of May, Norway celebrates National Constitution Day. It is the biggest national celebration of the year. The whole country is covered with Norwegian flags. Many homes have big flag posts in their garden and the flags flying make a beautiful sight. By mid May the trees are just starting to bud and a vague blanket of green is seen over the hills. Small birch trees are chopped down, tied in various places and decorated with flags in the centre of the villages. All the children are given brand new outfits for this event. The sound of snare drums, trumpets and clarinets ring throughout all the villages. Orchestras parade proudly with flag carriers, followed by huge parades of people singing traditional folksongs. After the parade, all sorts of games and competitions are held, almost like a funfair, and prizes can be won. This was a day I loved, but also hated.

Mum always sewed new clothes for the kids for this event and I always felt I looked very good and was proud to have something new. Mum ironed the flags kept from previous years and stuck a little ribbon the colour of the flags, red, blue and white, onto our coats. The girls' ribbons were fixed on the right side of the chest, Dad and Ted wore them on the left side of the chest.

We always had to be at the village, which was 8 miles away,

early in the morning to join our own school class, lining up to participate in the parade. First came the musicians, they were at the front, forming straight lines and wearing blue uniforms. Secondly, the school's first grade joined in behind the musicians and then all the other grades, up to the last year. The Primary School and the Comprehensive School held about 100 kids in total. In those days school didn't begin until you reached the age of seven and then you left school at the age of sixteen. Our Primary school was from the age of seven to the age of thirteen. At fourteen years old you entered the Comprehensive school and then left at sixteen. In our village all the children went to the same school because it was such a small community. In my class there were three girls and six boys, the nine kids were together in the same class for the whole of the nine years.

I dreaded the long walk of the parade. We walked right through the village, up a very steep bendy road to the top of a hill, (in Wales it would be called a mountain!). I had such a bad cough all the time. The walk would make me short of breath and then I would start to cough. To keep up with the fast speed of the parade was a nightmare, but it was compulsory to be in the parade when you were a school kid. Every kid that finished the parade had a free hot dog and a free bottle of pop. So for me not to starve all day I had to finish the parade and I always did, enjoying afterwards the lovely taste of a proper hot dog. This was a treat I had just once a year. Mum never had hot dogs for dinner.

While we were out and about, Mum and Dad would meet up with some friends from the village and have their own party. They would then sit with them and get drunk! Everywhere kids would be playing games and joining in races to win great prizes, but you had to pay about one Krone (10 pence) to be a part of each game. I never had any money so I just walked around looking at everyone else having fun. All the kids were stuffing their mouths with chocolates and ice-cream one after another. They competed over who had managed to eat the most sweets and ice creams. On this particular day of the year, that was the tradition, the kids were allowed to eat all the sweets they wanted.

I kept my bottle of pop for as long as I could, so it would look as if I had goodies too. But in the end I had no more pop and I was longing to have sweets like everyone else had. There was one race that I participated in that didn't cost money and that was the 3 wheeled bike race for toddlers. The organisers said I was too old for this race; this was only for the smaller ones! I was now seven years old but still very small. I pleaded with the organisers to please let me have a go! I was not that much taller than them. In the end they let me have a go. I was too tall to sit on the seat, so I sat at the back of the bike and raced as fast as I could so that I could get a prize of some sort. I won the race of course, and I got my prize! To my great disappointment it was a very big green apple. I took a bite out of it and it was not sweet at all, it was the sourest apple I had ever had.

From early in the morning until late afternoon, for most of the celebrations during the Norwegian Constitution Day, all I had was one small bottle of pop and one hot dog. Sometimes though I got very lucky and Mum would give me one Krone for one small ice cream. But the times when Granny was around during the celebrating of the Constitution were different. I stuck to her like Velcro, knowing she would always give me special treats, like ice creams and chocolates.

Chapter 12

BECOMING A THIEF

One time, when I was about seven and a half years old, I went with Granny to a small shop in the countryside. She bought a few items and was about to pay for them whilst busy talking with the cashier. They were chatting and laughing and didn't pay any attention to me. Suddenly, I saw an opportunity to grab a chocolate. I had gotten very tired of not having any money for sweets like the other kids. I was wearing a thick red coat. I saw a big roll of chocolate buttons by the till. I quickly snatched it and put it up the sleeve of my coat. My heart beat so fast, I thought it was going to pop out of my chest and I could not say a word when Granny turned around to talk to me. All I was thinking was that I had to get out of the shop before someone discovered what I had done!

Granny finished her shopping. We left the shop and jumped on the bus to go home. Even though my heart still beat fast with fright at what I had just done, I was amazed that I had managed to get a sweet without paying for it! With great excitement I opened my chocolate on the bus. Granny asked me, "How did you get that chocolate?" I blushed but was honest with her and said that I had just taken it from the shop. She started laughing and said, "Well done, my girl, you managed to steal that without been seen. Just make sure no one ever sees you, then you will get good at it!"

We both started giggling and had a laughing fit on the bus. I thought it was funny that Granny was so positive about my stunt. I loved my Granny so much. She always made me feel good about myself. It was so cool that she knew how to steal too! I broke off a piece of my chocolate to share with her, but I discovered the chocolate looked as though it had melted sometime before and now had turned white. I broke off another piece and started to eat it, but it tasted old and didn't taste like chocolate at all. I became very angry. I had been so nervous for nothing, and I thought to myself, I will never steal from that stupid shop again. I will steal from a shop that has fresh chocolate! Granny said not to worry, I would have better luck next time.

Stealing became a way of life for me from then on. I didn't need to go without sweets anymore! I became braver and braver each time I stole something. I also thought that my siblings would never laugh at their Christmas presents again, because now I had a way to find them something really nice.

As I grew older, I understood that some of the frustration Mum had with Granny was that Granny stole things from Mum. I also learned that she stole from most people she knew. Granny didn't keep what she stole, she gave things away, so she was not stealing because she needed the things, I think she was just addicted to stealing. She sometimes came home after shopping, pulling out a small roll of sellotape saying, "Look what I found on the floor in the shop, I just picked it up, thinking this is someone's rubbish."

*****

I had looked forward so much to starting school and I enjoyed my first day. But with only two other girls and six boys in my class it was difficult to make a friend. I lived in the countryside and the two girls lived on the same estate, by the school. For the first year I walked around in the school yard alone. I sometimes played on the swing and occasionally the other girls allowed me to play different games with them, although joining them in their games was a rare occurrence. It was a small school and the kids had already established friendships before they started school because most of them lived near to each other in the valleys. However, the farm that I came from had no kids nearby that were my age, so I became an outsider from day one.   I loved to be in class, though, learning to read and write, and my favourite lesson was drawing.

My Mum was a great cook, but there was one thing she was dreadful at and that was making bread. She put loads of sugar and salt into the dough, which did not complement each other. She rolled out huge rolls of bread, baking them in the oven on a very high heat. They were always burned black on the top and the crust underneath was as black and hard as coal. In the centre of the bread the dough was sometimes still uncooked. I brought sandwiches with me to school but could never eat much because of the horrible taste. In Norway there are no school kitchens where you can buy food; even today kids have to bring their own food. But I had become a very good thief. The only problem was that kids were not allowed to leave the school premises at any time. But I soon found a way to sneak off the yard, unseen, to get to the shop where I was able to steal chocolate. Sweets often became my lunch.

In my second year at school when I was eight years old, the whole school gathered in the gym hall. A dentist came in and held a lecture on how to look after our teeth. I was amazed at the effect a toothbrush could have on your teeth. I had never had a toothbrush and I went straight home and gave Mum the same lecture and said she had to get me a toothbrush too. I wanted to look after my teeth. Now I knew why I had toothache all the time and I needed to get some fillings done.

Mum had lost her teeth by the time she was 26, due, she thought, to all the pregnancies. I asked Mum when I was a child why she didn't have any teeth. She told me that she had thrown up so much during her pregnancies, her teeth had decayed. She couldn't afford to go to the dentist to have them fixed, so she ended up getting false teeth. After I became an adult, though, I heard Ted shouting at Dad that he had smashed all of Mum's teeth.

But for school children the dentist was free and I was able to go and have fillings done. To my surprise Mum got me a tooth brush, and I started to clean my teeth morning and night.

Chapter 13

I'D RATHER HAVE A FATHER I HATE, THAN NO FATHER AT ALL

Get the hell out of my house, you whore child, who do you f***ing think you are, you little bitch, look at those eyes, look at them everybody, check out those eyes of hers, can you see who she f***ing looks like? She's got Nicky's eyes, doesn't she? She doesn't belong here in this family with us, she is a f***ing whore child, get the hell out, get out of my sight, get out will you, go to hell, go over to Nicky's farm where you belong, you are just a whore child!"

My Dad's words roared throughout the sitting room as he pointed his finger at me, with eyes thundering in anger and hatred towards me. Just moments before, Dad had been playing his accordion! Mum could barely sit straight and her eyes were almost shut. I was just sitting there watching them, minding my own business, but knowing what was coming and it did.

It was always the same pattern, although I never got used to it. I lived with a false hope that Dad would forget and leave me alone. My body would be tensed up and I was not able to relax. My back, in particular, hurt all the time. I had grown out of my little cot. It was only about three feet long and it was too small for me. At eight years of age I was only 114 centimetres tall and very thin, weighing only 20 kilos, but I could not stretch out. I slept curled up on my side every night. I longed to sleep on my stomach because it was my favourite position. That way I was able to knock my head into the hard base of my cot to make myself fall asleep. But now trying to fall asleep I had to turn on my side after I had knocked my head, and because I had to change position it took me out of my spinning world.

My hope was shattered when Mum and Dad had their usual binge drinking, and now Dad was in his usual angry state. I knew each time he would start on me. I had gotten used to that. There was nowhere for me to go though. It was cold everywhere, so I always had to stay where my parents were if I didn't want to get cold. I was too scared of the dark house to go and hide anywhere. I knew Dad would not find me if I went to the attic and hid behind the rubbish and curtains there, but the attic was too scary. I felt evil up there, not to mention all the spiders that were hiding in the cobwebs.

"Why are you still sitting there, you f***ing bastard, I told you to get the hell out of my house, and get away from my sight." Dad was in a rage, swearing at me. "You are not my f***ing daughter, so piss off. Whore child, that's your name, and that is what you are." I used to sit still and just listen to him with my head down; now and again I would glance up to see his face filled with rage and anger.

But now I was eight years old and a bit braver. I had started to dare to defend myself by answering him back. I screamed whilst running for the door: "I am glad you are not my father. I am better off because I don't risk becoming like you. I have different genes then, I would hate to have such a f***ing monster of a dad like you, because I hate you, I hate you." My heart was beating fast and I had the feeling of a huge weight, like a heavy stone, sinking inside my chest. It was hard to breathe with this awful feeling, as if I was choking, at the same time trying not to cry. I thought he must not see me cry, because then he would think that I cared. I pressed my lips so tight together that they became one, convincing myself I don't need to cry, I don't need a father!

At the same time, other thoughts were racing through my mind. "Then who am I, and to whom do I belong? Why can't I belong to a family, why do I always have to be alone, who can I go to?" I felt as if I was forever being thrown into a deep muddy well, surrounded with darkness and dirt, with no light above and no way of getting out. And deep inside I didn't mean what I had shouted. I wanted Dad to be my father, even though I had grown to hate him. I would rather have a father I hated, than no father at all.

I ran upstairs to the bedroom and jumped into my cot and tried to hide under the blankets. I was shaking with fear and hoped it would be a long time before Mum and Dad came to bed. I was exhausted, hungry, cold and too afraid to fall asleep. I turned around on my stomach with my legs bent up at the bottom of my bed. I started as always, to knock my head into the hard base of my cot when I got tired of knocking my head I started to shake it sideways. This drifted me into the dizzy daze where my world was spinning again.

I don't know how long it took before Mum and Dad came stumbling into the room to go to bed. I lay there trying to become invisible, I hardly dared to breathe. I thought that if Dad saw my chest moving he would start again. They got into bed and Dad started to push Mum in the bed. She was so drunk I don't know if she at first felt him beating her, while shouting, "You f***ing whore, you slut, where is your f***ing lover now?" When she was drunk she always fought back to defend herself as best as she could. I don't know if she had sobered up at all on this occasion, but I saw her manage to claw Dad's face and pull out his hair. A full on fight was the normal pattern during their drinking rages and it often got worse in the bedroom, where they would scream and fight in their fury. At this stage I wouldn't dare to interfere; all I could do was lie still and try to breathe as little as possible.

The next morning I got up and quietly went downstairs. I entered the sitting room. It was covered with thick cigarette smoke and I found the house in a mess. Bottles everywhere and overflowing ashtrays. The room was still ice cold, they hadn't lit the fire. Mum sat in her chair with her feet resting on the coffee table, tilting the chair back. Her hands were shaking as she tried to drink a cup of coffee with one hand and hold a cigarette in the other. She was staring blankly and I could see her eyes were filled with emptiness. It was as if she lived in a different world, where only she existed.

Dad was sitting on the couch opposite, drinking a bottle of beer. He had far from sobered up, and as he lifted his hand to sip from the bottle, I saw his hands were shaking even more than Mum's. Mum's lower lip was split open, she had dark blue bruises on her face, and it was worse around her eyes. Dad's face was covered with scratch marks and the blood from that had dried into dark red scabs on his face. I said nothing to them. I didn't want to be seen. I saw that Dad was not drunk enough to start arguing yet, he had too big a hangover! So I knew I was on safe ground. I did not know how long this particular drinking season

would last. It depended on how much alcohol they had left, but
the pattern was always the same every time they drank

Chapter 14

GLINTS OF LIGHT

About once a week Mum and Dad went shopping. The nearest shop was 8 miles away. I always nagged, begged, and pleaded to go with them but very rarely was I allowed to go. They used to sneak off. I wouldn't know they were gone or where they were, until they came home with loads of shopping bags. On occasion I remember going outside the house, only to see Mum and Dad hurrying into the car, slamming the car doors, and driving off down the road, with me running after the car shouting, "Wait for me, wait for me, I want to come." I would see Ted's head in the back window, poking his tongue out at me and giving me his devilish look. Hours later when they came back, Ted would boast about all the chocolate he had been given and ice-cream too, and then he would say, "I get everything, you get nothing because you are the whore child and not worth a shit. I am so glad you get nothing because I hate you."

On the few occasions I was allowed to go with Mum shopping, Mum would stop for a coffee at the local bakery. Mum never ate much and would just have coffee with cream on the side. With all the lovely smells coming from the bakery I would beg her to buy me a Danish pastry. She always absolutely refused and would say, "Here's some cream left over from my coffee, drink that." I would catch a glimpse of the face of the woman who was running the bakery, going from a big smile, to a face of pity. At one time I heard her say to Mum, "Look, I do have some lovely pastries from yesterday, there are at least 10 of them in the bag. I normally sell each pastry for 3 Krone (30 pence), but I can let you have the whole bag for only 5 Krone (50 pence). Don't tell anyone I sold them to you so cheaply, but then your kid can have a taste." Mum said a firm no thanks, quickly drank her coffee and we left the shop.

The strangest thing though, is that when I was allowed to go shopping with Dad, and those occasions were few and far between, it was totally different. Dad would go to the petrol station to fill up with petrol and have a chat with his mate who ran the station. I had to wait a long time before he was ready to go home. In those days the petrol stations were like garages where they also fixed cars. They were not grocery stores like today, the only extra they had in the petrol stations were bottles of pop and ice creams.

I remember asking Dad in the nicest way I could, if I could please have an ice cream. I was allowed to choose the ice cream I wanted. In those brief moments, when Dad bought me an ice cream, I felt like I had a dad! Enjoying my ice cream, I felt very good and happy, not just because the taste of the ice cream was wonderful, but the fact that it was Dad himself who had bought it for me, and I didn't have to nag to get it. I believe Dad must have wanted me to have it! A warm feeling flowed through my whole body and I held on to those few moments as if they were precious gold. Receiving any kind of affection from my Dad was so rare, I have never forgotten them. When Dad was sober he never treated me bad in any way, by calling me names or wanting to throw me out. He was far more generous than Mum, and I was never afraid of him when he didn't drink.

Chapter 15

FEER OF DARKNESS

I was kneeling down, a small bundle in the middle of the road during a winter blizzard, waiting to die. I was only eight years old. My eyes were tightly shut. I plugged my ears with my fingers, plunging them deeply into my ears. I didn't want to hear if a car was approaching. All I wanted was for my life to be over. My mind was taken over by darkness and despair. My body was covered with bruises from Ted's beatings. There had been no rest from his beatings for a long time. I could not take it any longer and I found no other hope for escape but to end my life.

Suddenly I heard a voice. "Hey kid, what on earth are you doing out here in the middle of the road? Don't you see it's a blizzard? I could have hit you, it's a miracle I saw you in time." I slowly turned around and lifted my head with considerable embarrassment, thinking to myself, I sure hope he doesn't know what I was about to do! I felt totally exposed. The bus driver stood right behind me with the bus he had abruptly stopped just three feet from where I was sitting. His face was covered with tears, as he continued to say, "I could have hit you, I could have hit you with my bus, quickly, get out of here, go home." I got up on my feet and started to walk towards home, glad he didn't start to question me further about what I had wanted to do. I turned around and could barely look at him, while he was shaking his head, before he went back onto the bus and drove off.

I had to return to the house of hell, failing in my attempt to die. More and more my heart felt like it was turning into stone. I did not know how I would be able to continue to cope with it all. With slow steps I walked towards the house, uncertain when Ted was going to attack next. I quietly went up to the bedroom and threw myself down in my cot, I just stared at the ceiling, thinking this was not my real life, that it was just a dream and that I would soon wake up from it. I wished that I was a little bird, with wings that could fly high above all the mountains, far away from this house.

*****

In Norway in the seventies, if the amount of alcohol in a drunken driver's blood was found to be more than 0.5 per thousand, he was considered under the influence. Today there is zero tolerance. In 1975 when I was nine years old, Dad had started to work as a bus driver about 95 miles away, with Fjords and Ferries. Dad was unable to come home from work every day. Mary had left home by now, so there were only four of us left. Sally was going to leave that summer. Dad commuted home every weekend and Mum was left to tend to all the work on the farm. Sometimes Mum went to see Dad at weekends. There she had access to more alcohol, since this was a city and it was easy to get.

Mum and Dad had both been drinking and driving and caught by the police.

Mum lost her driving license and got a fine. She didn't want to pay the fine, so she went to jail instead. I don't know how many days Mum was in jail, but she went and came back. I didn't notice any difference if she was at home or if she was not, I had become very apathetic by now. I simply didn't care. Later Dad was caught drinking and driving. He put up a big argument with the police and said he was innocent; he ended up in jail too. But not for long!

I remember the two policemen that came to our house to question Dad. He had been drinking that day and he really thought he had a brilliant idea. Dad had hidden Sally's cassette player on the shelf under the coffee table, to get evidence that the police were "lying"! Only God knows why he thought that would help him with his case. When the police arrived there was mayhem in the house, but I felt relieved that this time the shouting was not directed at me. When the police eventually left, Dad was celebrating his victory over them. The fact that he had recorded his conversation with the police without them knowing it, made me think Dad was clever and very brave to even dare to do that, and I felt a slight admiration for him at that moment.

Their drinking continued for days, Mum and Dad of course fought with each other on and off. Suddenly Dad was shouting for Sally, running around the house slamming all the doors so they almost jumped off their hinges. "Where is the bloody cassette player, and where are the f***ing tape recordings?" Sally had taken back her cassette player and accidentally recorded pop music over Dad's interview with the police.

Dad was furious and stormed into Sally's room in the attic, grabbed her player, all her cassettes and ran downstairs with them. When he entered the sitting room he opened the door of the fire stove and threw the lot in. The stove was not lit and he turned around to get some newspaper so that he could light a fire. I saw my moment, wanting to help Sally, and snatched the cassette player out of the stove and ran to the hallway. Dad was drunk, so he was not quick enough to grab me when I took off and I headed upstairs to the second floor. But when I was on the twelfth step of the stairs, Dad managed to reach for my feet as he had made it to the hall. The stairs had no outer rail, so when you were downstairs and as tall as an adult you could almost reach up to the top of the stairs.

With a bang, my head hit the top step as my Dad pulled my feet from underneath me. My head bounced hard on each step as he dragged me down to where he was standing. I know I passed out for a couple of seconds and I woke up to Dad beating me all over my body. I screamed hysterically and again I saw out of the corner of my eye Mum just standing there at the end of the hall, watching Dad beat me up. "Help me, help me!" I screamed, but nothing was done.

I was so hysterical, I must have spun around uncontrollably, because I managed to slip out of Dad's grip and run into the kitchen and from there into the sitting room. Dad was running after me, so I ran back out into the other hallway and around and around he chased me. I thought he would catch me soon and I needed to run outside if I didn't want to be caught again. I was terrified of the dark, but headed for the door, with Dad just a few feet away. I ran down the road with him chasing me, screaming, "I'll get you, you bloody kid. I will beat the life out of you." I ran down to the main road as fast as I could. It felt like an eternity. It was pitch black, no moonlight or stars to give any light. Afterwards I realised it was good there was no moonlight that night, because Dad would have been able to see where I was!

I had to get off the main road and run across the fields. Dad was not far behind me! I shot off the road towards the neighbouring farm. The place where I ran off the road was swamplike, because of the overflow of silage and the open sewerage from their farm. I heard Dad's voice shouting, and suddenly my right foot stuck in the deep mud! I pulled with all the strength I had left to get out. Finally I was loose, but one of my slippers was sucked into the mud hole. I continued to run up the hill without my slipper, not realizing that Dad was not shouting anymore. He had given up running after me. I finally reached the neighbouring farm, but was so out of breath that I was unable to speak for a while.

The neighbours took me in and they didn't dare to send me home that night, so they gave me a bed and said that I could wait until the next day before going home when hopefully Dad would have sobered up. This was the only time I had gone to someone outside the home for help. My whole world revolved around the house. To me everything further than 200 yards was too far to go, and hitchhiking I had only done a few times during daytime. I never thought I could get help from anyone before, because everyone lived so far from the house and it was too scary to go out in the night. Although I hadn't planned to run to the neighbouring farm that night, it was the only option I had, to avoid being caught by Dad. Without thinking, I just ran out into the dark, scary night. It was only when I was running away from him that the thought struck me that I could run up to the neighbours' white house on the hill.

Dad eventually had to go back to the city to work when his weekends were over. With Dad gone, Mum started to have a man visiting her now and again during the mid week. He was a lovely guy. He rang Mum and asked if he could take me to dinner in the local village, 9 miles away. So he picked me up, we went to eat, and after we had eaten we went home to Mum. She and he would then normally disappear and I was left to sort myself out. I knew something was going on, but I didn't care. This was a nice man, he took me out for dinner to a proper hotel every week, and I loved it!

It was a better season for me. Dad was working far away and a new man was coming to the house, making me feel special. He took me for dinner and not Angela or Ted. This secret life that Mum was living went on for about a year.

Chapter 16

MUM LEAVING DAD

In the summer of 1976 when I was ten years old, my uncle and auntie from Denmark were visiting. They had grown up in the West of Norway where skiing is a must at wintertime. Uncle missed skiing terribly, so when he was back in Norway on holiday he just had to go skiing. Denmark has no mountains. It is very flat and there is rarely any snow during the winter. Each year, when Uncle came home, he looked for a place that had snow. In Norway even in summertime there is plenty of snow left over at the foot of the mountains. But you really need to climb to at least 2000 ft to get to the snow. Uncle once asked me if I wanted to go with him on a hike, so that he could ski on the snow before it thawed. We parked the car at Granny's sister's house and off we went.

It was a very hot summer day and he carried his skis on his shoulders. We walked for many hours before we reached the place where he could go cross country skiing. This place had no access by car; it had to be reached on foot. I didn't know at the time where we were, but it was far into the wilderness. As an adult, when I look towards the mountains where we went, I can see that it was a very long walk.

We finally reached a place where there was quite a lot of snow, but it was on the other side of the river. Uncle said, "It's brilliant here. I can ski for a while on this patch, let me just cross the river first." Uncle decided to cross the river although it was still partly covered with snow. I asked if it was safe, as the snow was pretty soft. He said, "Just wait here and I'll give it a try." He had almost reached the other side of the river, when the snow he was standing on broke loose from the edge and he sailed down the stream a few metres. I was so afraid that he would be taken by the river. I feared he could get cramp if he fell in and would not be able to swim because of the ice cold water. I knew it would have been impossible for me to run for help, because I realized that I had not paid attention to where we were going. I had just followed uncle on this endless walk into the mountains.

The big chunk of snow that he was trapped on suddenly smashed into the riverbank further down the stream. My uncle threw himself forward towards the bank, where he plunged his snow stick into the riverside and pulled himself out onto the bank. I was left on the other side, relieved that he was on dry land. Uncle shouted across to me that I should walk downstream, keep my eyes on him, and follow him down the valley. I couldn't always see my uncle because of the terrain; the trees and bushes often blocked him from my sight. Scared stiff at being lost made me focus and do what he said. Eventually, he found a spot where the river was not too deep and had no dangerous snow covering. He crossed over by climbing on the rocks that rose above the water. Then we took the long walk back down the valley to some of our relatives. It was not until I got older that I realized that Uncle could have lost his life, if he had fallen into the ice cold river, and I would never have found my way home from where I was.

We arrived at our relative's house. To my surprise, my mum was there with Aunt Sara. Also Nan from up North had been visiting us that summer. This had led to a lot of arguments between Nan and Dad. The two seemed not to be able to stand each other. Now they were all together at this relative's house! Mum never visited relatives at all, because they were Granny's relatives anyway. She didn't like visiting the different farms in the area because Mum said that they were all gossipers, so I found it strange that Mum was there.

Mum said to me, "There you are. We have been waiting hours for you and now we have to hurry." I was totally exhausted, very thirsty and hungry. I hadn't eaten all day and to have been on such a long hike without food was unbearable. The relatives gave me a slice of bread that I truly enjoyed, but I noticed that the adults around me were whispering.

When I had eaten, Mum said, "Come on, we are going up to the north of Norway." I jumped up as fast as I could in excitement and happiness, so glad we were going on a holiday. I asked Mum, "Where is Dad, and the others, and where is our car?" Mum said, "They are not coming, we are going alone with Nan and they don't know we are leaving. I am leaving Dad. Quickly, come, we've got to go before Dad tries to find us."

I got even more excited when she said that. She was leaving Dad and I could not wait to go. I became very excited. This was just like a movie, very scary, and I was in it. I just hoped that it was true, not like the last time, about a year earlier. Mum had said she wanted to leave Dad. She was really drunk when she said it and she could hardly sit up straight. Angela, Ted and I sat in the living room with Mum and we were trying to comfort her in the best way we knew how. She really wanted to leave him. She sobbed like a little child, "Where can I go and where can I get money for me to survive? I can't take this anymore. I am going crazy, my nerves can't take it any longer."

I had secretly saved up some money for a while and I had 10 Krone (1 pound) in my pocket. I treasured it like gold because I had also started to save up for my own escape. It was a big risk for me to say I had money, because Ted would probably try to steal it from me. I had had 10 Krone before and it just disappeared after I had showed it to Ted. But I thought it is better for Mum to have this than me and then we all could get out of here. I said to Mum, "Here take this money. It will help us to leave and I am sure that will be enough for some food." She said that it was not enough to live on and that there was nothing that she could do to get away. Slowly Mum fell asleep and the next day things went back to normal. Mum was sobered up and she didn't leave.

Now, on this fine, hot summer morning and after 18 years of marriage, Mum left Dad and she went back home, up North, and she took only me with her out of all of her kids. Mary and Sally had moved out by then and were living on their own, so it was only Angela and Ted left home with Dad. I was over the moon with happiness. I was off and away from this hell, a new hope and a future ahead of me.

Nan had paid for our ticket to go with her up North and she was very happy on the trip back home. It was a two day journey on a ship before we arrived there. Nan was very happy to have her daughter back home and everything seemed to go my way. When we arrived Mum sorted out our rooms at Nan's house. Nan had an upstairs apartment, but there was no toilet there, so we had to go downstairs into a very dark and muddy basement where Nan's old toilet was located. Nan was very fussy and didn't want anyone to use the toilet that was located in her part of the house. There would be too many germs with us using hers!

The weekend came and Mum and I went straight to Wilma's house. Very soon more and more people came to Wilma's house, carrying big bags of alcohol. Then the party began. Later in the night, Wilma asked me if I could look after her twin boys and her other little son. Her baby sitter had let her down and she thought I would do a good job. She bought us loads of sweets that we could enjoy, but the sweets made us all very hyper. I was ten years old, and the twins Robert and Richard were six, and the little one, Rick, was four. I felt very proud to be asked to babysit; it made me feel like a real adult. All the adults went out to party and I was left in charge of three other small children.

The twins were a real handful as they ran around the house. I tried to catch them as they were running wild. When I caught one, the other twin set a trap to help his brother out of my grip and off they went laughing, round and round. Then I made a plan of how to get them to go to bed. I said, "We shall play circus and you can be the audience, but you must lie in bed while I entertain you." All three of them agreed, and they sat expectant in their beds. I played the part of a circus artist, jumping up and down in Wilma's bed, as high as I could, waving my night dress up and down, showing them my bum, to make the boys laugh. I ended the show by showing how brave I was, throwing myself backwards, down onto the soft mattress. It was probably 11pm and I had managed to put the four year old into his cot, where he giggled himself off to sleep. After my performance, though, the twins did not keep their promise to go to sleep. They jumped out of bed and the chase started all over again. Catching the twins was like playing cowboys and Indians. Finally I persuaded them that if they came to bed I would read fairytales to them. Once I had done one fairytale they promised to be quiet, but as soon as I had finished the story, they jumped out of bed and ran around. Then I had to persuade them again with the promise of another fairytale, and about four stories later, they were finally asleep. I plunged down in my own bed, totally exhausted after the evening's events and fell fast asleep.

I didn't see much of Mum during those first weeks up North. Mum went binge drinking every day. I was left to care for myself and was out of the house all day. Nan gave me breakfast and out I went, to try to find friends. I met a couple of girls down the street that I got to know a little bit and I liked them very much. They were six years older than me. I was so proud that they talked to me when I was only ten. I guess they felt sorry for me being alone all the time, so they spoke to me when I was out in the streets. One of the girls told me that there was a circus in town that day and if I wanted to go with them I could. The girls said they were going to see all the handsome boys at the circus.

I was over the moon, but I remembered the next door neighbour had a daughter who was one year older than me and she had already invited me to her birthday. I was so happy, because I had never been invited to a birthday party before. I was torn between the two events and I knew Mum would not give me money for both, so I said, "I can't make it, there is this birthday I am going to." The girl said, "Look, if the birthday finishes early just pop in and we will take you to the circus too."

I went to Mum for money so that I could give it as a present. Luckily Mum gave me ten Krone and I put it in an envelope, and wrote happy birthday on the outside. I did not have a card or anything, because I had nothing to make a card with, all my pencils and sheets were left at home in the west. My heart was bouncing with excitement and I was very nervous as I carefully rang the doorbell of her house. I was the first one to arrive. I entered a big, beautiful home. I looked around and saw it was new and very clean. Their living room was L-shaped and it had large windows that faced the most beautiful garden, with lovely rosebushes and fruit trees placed perfectly around the nicely cut lawn. Their living room had so many nice decorations and lovely paintings on the walls. There was a big dining table filled with all sorts of lovely cakes and candies in the corner of this huge room. My mouth watered as I looked at all the sweets I could not wait to taste.

Soon the living room filled with girls smelling lovely. They all were wearing nice dresses and had lovely necklaces around their necks. Some of them also had beautiful nail varnish. The girls began giggling, holding their hands in front of their mouths, as they gazed towards me, checking me out from top to bottom. I didn't wear a dress and I only owned two pairs of trousers. I was wearing the pair I thought was the nicest. They were home sewn and I had an ordinary sweater on. I realised I couldn't remember the last time I had had a bath! I had brushed my hair, but it felt sticky and I suddenly noticed my trousers were very dirty. All these clean girls made me realise how dirty I was.

I thought to myself, they won't think of my clothes or how dirty I am when they see my very generous gift. I proudly handed the envelope to the birthday girl. I thought it was a wonderful treat for her to get ten Krone. This was a huge sacrifice for me; it cost me the ticket for the circus. I had never had so much money given to me at once before. I was waiting for a huge gasp of surprise from the girls when they saw how generous I was. But when she opened the envelope and found the ten Krone inside, she turned around to the rest of the girls and waved the coin in the air. "Look at this, girls, look at this. Ten stupid Krone! Ha! Ha! Come to a birthday party with only ten stupid Krone and not even a card. Mum told me to invite her. I didn't want that girl here, then I thought I could invite her to get a gift from her, but look at this stupid ten Krone. You can get nothing for ten Krone, nothing that I want at least." They all laughed and I was speechless and embarrassed. If there had been a hole in the floor I would have jumped into it. I felt my face go hot and I knew I blushed very red.

Suddenly I felt something inside me rise up. I don't know if a defense mechanism kicked in but it triggered a train of thought that went through my head. In my mind I was thinking, "I wasted my ten Krone and my chance to go to a circus on this spoiled brat. She is a stupid, spoiled girl with freckles, and she is so ugly--her face is fat and her eyes look like holes in a letterbox and her lips are so fat that she could stumble in them while she is walking, and she speaks with a lisp. She is a rich kid who treats people bad. She is just an arse not to appreciate my gift. Who does she think she is? I am leaving this stupid party, and I don't want to have friends that make me look like a fool."

With those thoughts, I said to the girl, "I've got to go now; I don't have time to be here any more because I have been invited to go to the circus with the big girls down the street and I am going to have a lot more fun than here. Bye." I saw a big gasp of surprise on her face when I said I was going with the big girls, and with a smile on my face I ran out of the door feeling I had the victory because I had proof that even if it seems that you have "everything", you don't have "everything" if that "everything" makes you an arse. I thought to myself, I am doing just fine by having nothing. I don't want to be around people like that. No one had ever taught me any manners, but I knew I would never treat anyone like that and make a fool of someone in front of people. Relieved not to be around those people, I ran off down the street to find the girls that were going to the circus.

I ran down the street to find the older girls who were just about to leave. "Hey, Laila, good you could make it." It was a fair walk to the circus and I had no money for the ticket, but I went to the circus grounds anyway. It turned out that none of us had any money for the tickets; we were all sneaking around and climbing fences to look at everything. The big girls gasped at the handsome boys and I thought they looked good too, but I was not interested in boys then. I felt like I was a part of a big adventure just to be around the big girls, and I felt accepted for who I was, and not just a dirty, little unwanted girl.

*****

During this time, Mum often locked herself away in Nan's upstairs apartment drinking. I remember being hungry a lot during those months. When I was hungry and wanted food, I would knock and knock at her door. Suddenly, a stranger, a tall man with a big beard, opened the door and told me to leave them alone and piss off. I said, "Who are you? I want my Mummy, I need food." The stranger pushed me away, slammed the door in my face, and locked me out. I didn't see her at all. She was drunk inside the room. She had been drinking for weeks and I never saw her sober. I felt furious about the man who had taken Mum. That was how I felt. He had taken Mum, now that she was free from Dad.

I liked the man who had come to our house secretly, when we lived back home. Mum seemed happy around him and he treated her nicely. He was kind to me and gave me pocket money. Sometimes he took me to a restaurant. But this man was different, there was something scary about him. I felt he had stolen Mum, and she didn't know it, and I felt she was in a worse prison here than back home.

I continued to kick and scream at the door for this stupid stranger to let me in, but without result. The man came and went many times and I didn't like him at all; he never let me in. Then weeks went by, and I didn't see him anymore. I was relieved to finally have access to the apartment again. But suddenly, there was another man who started coming and going and I was again denied entry to the apartment to see my mum. I thought these stupid men had no right to take my Mum. She was not theirs to own. I remember Mum complaining to Dad when she was drunk, "I am tired of being your slave. I am tired of being your whore." But now she allowed those men to come to her and do the same and I felt it was worse, because they were strangers, they were not Dad. She was married to Dad and not to them. I wondered why she gave herself away to them. I was only ten years old, but I knew she was having sex with them, and I knew it was wrong.

I began to go to Nan instead. She fed me and I gave up trying to get Mum's attention or to get her away from those men. I pretty much minded my own business. I was getting to know some more girls further down the street, and we played in the playgrounds all day. Two months went by with Mum going on like this until one day Wilma told Mum she needed to get her act together. "You need to start a new and better life here. Why did you come back up to the North if you are going to be drunk all the

time? What kind of life is that? Look, we can have parties at the
weekends and have fun then, but not throughout the week too,"
she said. Wilma and Mum had a great relationship as sisters and
Mum knew Wilma was right. She knew she was ruining her life
with all the alcohol and all the boyfriends.

After their conversation Mum decided to sober up. She went
out to look for work and she got a job as a cleaner. She worked
hard from early in the morning till late in the afternoon. I often
went along to help her clean, so that the job would be finished
earlier and she could earn more.

One day I followed Mum to town where she was doing some
shopping. We passed a toy shop window with two Barbie dolls
on display. The two dolls looked very different, one was pretty
and one was ugly. The ugly one cost ten Krone, but the other one
that was so beautiful cost 15 Krone. The Barbie dolls were new
in Norway then and I wanted one so much. I begged Mum to buy
me a doll. I negotiated with her to give me the pretty doll. "Look
Mum, I don't have a single toy here. My big baby doll is at home
in the west, and I have nothing to play with here. I am a big girl
now and I don't want to play with a big baby doll anyway. Please,
I want a Barbie with long legs, one that has breasts. And, by the
way I have helped you on your two cleaning jobs and worked
hard, so you must give me this pretty Barbie doll."

Mum said she couldn't afford the more expensive one, but
she bought me the ugly one for ten Krone. I really hated the face
on the cheaper doll and I didn't like her, she was so ugly, but I
thought it would do. She had long legs and breasts that was the
most important part. It was better to have an ugly doll than no
doll at all! The following Christmas I was over the moon with
excitement when my Granny gave me the exact same doll as the

beautiful one I had seen in the shop window and my auntie Wilma sent me one exactly the same, too. Now I had two beautiful twin Barbie's and one ugly one.

When I played with the three dolls, the two beautiful dolls always hit and kicked the ugly one and gave it a hard time. I just hated the ugly doll. I liked to put the ugly doll on the floor and squeeze her head flat with my hand and whilst she was lying down I would take the pretty dolls' feet and kick her. A great anger would rise up within me when I was playing. I would lift the doll and hit her repeatedly onto the floor, not so much that she would break, but as much as I felt the doll deserved, shouting "You are a whore, no one wants you, get out of here, you deserve to be kicked. You are ugly, I hate you, I hate you, why are you still in my house? Why do I have to see your ugly face, you are just a bastard." I felt a great anger and hatred towards the ugly doll and I didn't know why I hated her, I just did! Sometimes now I search through my little box in the attic where I have kept the toys from my childhood, and funnily enough, the doll that I treated so cruelly is still there and not broken.

Mum seemed to be getting it together with work and all, with the result that I started to enjoy my stay up North. I had found a girl one year younger than me who I loved to play with. I wasn't beaten by anyone and I didn't feel so lonely. I sometimes went to the local shop down the street from Nan. I had saved some money, thanks to the people that partied at Wilma's house at weekends. They sometimes gave me money when they were really drunk, so I was able to save as much as I could to get enough for an ice-cream or a bottle of pop.

One day the lady that owned the shop whispered to me to come and have a talk with her. She said, "Laila, you need to come down to my house at six o'clock tonight. Your Dad rang me and he wants to talk to you. Your oldest sister wants to talk to you too; she has been in a car accident." The shop owner said my sister was doing fine, but she had stayed for a few days in hospital.

My heart raced through my chest. "What does Dad want to talk to me for?" I thought to myself. I was so scared, but at the same time excited that Dad wanted to talk to me and I was curious to find out how my sister was doing. The lady at the shop told me to tell no one about our conversation and to let no one know that I was going to her house to receive this phone call.

The time came and I went to the lady's house. I waited with excitement for the phone call from Dad. The phone rang and Mary's voice was on the other end. She told me she was okay, but she said she could have been killed in the car accident. She had been very lucky to survive. Then she told me that I had to come home to stay with Dad. I told her that I didn't want to go home. I reminded her that Ted regularly beat me up and Dad was always cruel to me when he was drunk. I said I wanted to stay here where I had friends that I could play with.

Then Mary told me that if I came home she would make sure that Ted never laid a hand on me again. She said, "Not only that, you have to think of the future. Think of Granny and Granddad. They are getting older you know, they are not going to live forever. Don't you want to see them again before they die, wouldn't you rather be with them than with Mum?" That made me think. I really missed Granny and Granddad and I really wanted them right now!

Then Dad came on the phone. "Laila," he said, "you have to come home to be with your Dad. This is where you belong, here with us. Your life is not up North, it's here. You must come back to Dad and Tally is missing you. She wags her tail when I mention your name." The words were like hymns to my ears. My Dad wanted me, I could not believe it! I knew Mary well enough to know that Ted would never dare to try it out on her, so when she said she would make sure Ted wouldn't beat me again, I believed that if anyone could put a stop to his abuse it would be her.

The joy I felt in my heart was overwhelming, with a deep longing to see Granny and Granddad and Tally, my dear dog. Oh how much I loved her! I was still not sure though, so I hesitated. Dad kept ringing in secret, several times a week, to try to persuade me to go home and it sure was working. Soon I decided to do all I could to try to get back home. I started to nag Mum to go home. I was longing for Granny and Granddad more and more and I had started to hate it at Nan's house. She was so mean and I didn't like her. I preferred to be at Auntie Wilma's house, who was always good to me.

On one occasion when we came home from town, Mum, Nan and I walked up the stairs to Nan's door. I was crying to Mum saying that I wanted to go home. Suddenly, Nan turned around, grabbed my arm, squashed it really hard and turned her face towards me. She then gurgled a big cough to collect spit from the back of her throat and spat right into my face, followed with shouts of, "That evil kid, she is nothing but trouble. Shut up, you are nothing but a spy." As usual, Mum said nothing to Nan for spitting in my face or calling me evil. I felt nothing but loathing for Nan then, and I thought to myself, Granny would never do anything thing like that to anyone in the whole world!

Soon the school holidays came to an end and I had not been enrolled in the new school. One day Mum just packed up all our stuff and suddenly we were on the same big ship that had brought us up North and on our way back to the West. While I lay in the bed on the boat, I thought how wonderful it would be to see Granny and Granddad again and I imagined Tally when she saw me, running towards me and jumping up 'til I fell over and then licking my face all over. Then I finally would have a Dad too, like every one else, because Dad had said on the phone that I belonged there with him!

The schools had started back one month before. Mum had finally given in to Dad's request to send me home and get me back to my own school. I also think it was Mary's car accident that worried Mum very much, even though Mary had moved from home two years earlier. She probably wanted to find out for herself that Mary was okay. When Dad rang to tell us that Mary was in hospital, Mum cried, but she tried to hide her tears. Mum never showed her emotions to anyone when she was sober, so when I saw her crying, I knew she was hurting.

Arriving at the docks in the West, my Aunt Sara and Dad were there to meet us. I was very nervous about meeting Dad again and I didn't know how to act or behave towards him. I didn't know how this new Dad stuff would work. When I saw Dad, he had grown a big long black beard. He had made a vow not to cut his beard 'til he got his driving licence back, the one he lost through drinking and driving. I thought he looked very old and didn't look like Dad at all.

Sara had an old beetle car and Mum was riding in the front with her, while Dad and I sat in the back seat. It was a 60 mile trip to our home. On those roads it took about two and a half hours to get back to the farm.   As soon as Aunt Sara started to head for home, Dad started his abuse towards Mum. He had obviously been drinking and he was overwhelmed with jealousy about Mum's departure from him months earlier. He started to pull her hair from the back seat and big lumps of Mum's hair came out in Dad's hands whilst he was shouting what a f***ing whore and a slut she was. Mum was sober and sat still in the front seat not saying one word the whole trip. He abused her all the way home. I sat as still as I could in the car and once again I tried to make myself invisible. My heart felt as if it had sunk into my belly, and I felt I had made a big mistake nagging Mum to come home. I couldn't hold back my tears and I cried without a sound as I felt very guilty to have brought Mum back to Dad. I didn't know that Mum had planned to just bring me home and then go back up North. She had not planned to stay, just a short trip to drop me off and get some of her clothes.

Finally we arrived home and it was then I found out that Mum was going to leave again the next day. I was so confused. I was home, glad that I was going to see Granny and Granddad whom I had missed so much, but I didn't want Mum to leave. The next morning Mum suddenly came smiling down the stairs. Dad was also smiling and they were both sober. They told Angela, Ted and me to come downstairs as they wanted to speak with us. When we all sat down, Dad said, "Mum and I have made up, I am not going to hit her anymore and I will treat her right. Mum is not leaving us again. Everything will be different from now on."

I felt a huge relief come over me and I was so happy, because I thought finally we would be like an ordinary family. Little did I know, now that Dad had to behave and be nice to Mum, that I was the one whose future would get much worse at home, much worse than I had known before! Dad targeted me more than he had ever done before, because I was not only a whore child but also a traitor that had left! He simply needed someone to pour out the terrible anger and jealousy he felt.

Later I asked Angela what made Mum change her mind. Mum had said to Angela, "There is no point in me staying here because no one loves me, all my kids despise me, so you all are better off without me." Angela said she answered Mum, "It is not true Mum. I love you, I care about you, I don't want you to leave." Perhaps those words penetrated Mum's heart and made her change her mind about leaving. I think she saw a new hope in that her kids did love her and want her.

Chapter 17

CRUSHED DREAMS

I was happy that Mum and Dad chose to stay together, and I thought things would get better from then on. They did for a while. I was also very nervous about going back to my school on the first day, after being absent for a whole month and into the first term of my 5th grade. I was relieved when my teacher said to me, "Welcome home, Laila. It is so good to have you back here with us." A warm feeling of acceptance swept over me, as if a warm blanket had been wrapped around me. I experienced much more joy in school during the next term. I became friends with a girl and we had a lot of fun together. We had reached the beginning of the giggling age!

Mum and Dad didn't drink for a while and things were quite normal. Granny and Granddad also stayed for longer periods of time at the farm. I was so happy to have Granny and Granddad there with me and I asked Granny if I could sleep in their room, since I had grown even further out of my own cot. I was sleeping in my cot at the age of ten, even though I had started to grow out of it at the age of eight. Granny had given her bedroom in the attic back to Mum and Dad. The room they were sleeping in now was their guest room and it was much bigger. It had three beds, but the spare bed was filled with a load of things that Granny had stacked away. She cleaned out all the boxes and bags, and prepared a lovely bed for me. I loved sleeping in their bedroom with them. The lovely smell of coffee in the morning announced that a new day had come. I felt so safe and comfortable with them.

As Christmas approached, Granny and Granddad went back to live with Sara. They knew it was the season where it was not safe to be around the farm. I dreaded them going, but I thought to myself, I am a good hitch hiker and I can visit them every weekend. Anyway, it was only 25 miles away and I had hitchhiked since I was six years old to visit them on weekends. But Christmas came and went and there was no trouble between Mum and Dad.

Dad did keep his word to leave Mum alone. But he started to express a growing hatred towards me. When he was drinking and got drunk, he would stretch out his arm full length and point towards me, shouting "Look at her!" His eyes were almost shut as he squeezed them together, despising me. "You, you, look at me when I am talking to you. Look at you, you f***ing whore child. Those eyes, look at the eyes of that bastard sitting over there. It's Nicky's eyes she got, isn't it, yeah, Nicky's eyes. What in the hell are you doing in my house? Get the hell out of here will you, did you not hear me, are you deaf too? Look at her, look at that girl, a fool as well, that is what she is, a f***ing fool. She was the only one that left Dad. Yeah, that proves to me you are not my daughter because, if you had stayed, I would have known you were loyal to me, and there could have been a chance you were of my blood. But you are not my f***ing daughter, you are the f***ing daughter of Nicky. Get out, get out. Get out of my f***ing sight before I kill you."

I felt total numbness, my heart was racing in my chest, ready to explode. The lump in my throat felt like it was choking me and I could hardly breathe. The adrenaline rushed through my body until I felt as if I were fainting. All I wanted was to disappear! I had lived in the hope that things were going to be okay, but Dad had revealed to me he didn't want me, he still thought I was not his daughter.

I was crying on the inside, wishing Granny was there. I ran into the kitchen and hid far under the kitchen table where Tally was sleeping with the cat on their rug. I curled up in between them and held the cat tightly, as Tally slowly lifted her head to see me lying down. I placed my head next to Tally and as I cried in silence my tears rolled down wetting her fur. Tally had been my only comfort so many times before, whenever I felt alone and totally abandoned. When I felt Tally's warm body next to me it gave me a feeling of safety. Knowing Tally would never hurt me, she would never abandon me, she was my true friend and she loved me.

Dad raged throughout the house slamming every door he went through, shouting "Where is that f***ing bastard, where is she gone? To hell I hope she has gone, yeah to hell".

I didn't move for hours, I just lay there waiting for this storm to be over, hoping I was invisible and wouldn't be found. I started to think to myself, I should never have nagged Mum to bring me home, this is worse than it was before! I thought I would have to wait now till I leave school before I could get away from this place, but I needed to find a way to get money.

The storms came and went throughout the year. I was safe when there was no alcohol around and Ted's pleasure in beating me had diminshed, as he found more interesting things to do. I tried to stay out of his way as much as I could. I played with my toys, in places where he could not find me. Ted started to get into fights at school, where he became one of the most feared boys to go near. Even the teachers could not cope with his violence. He even attacked them on occasions.

I had made a decision from a very young age never to steal from friends and family, only from shops. I had been a thief since I was six, but I wanted to be an "honest" thief, someone people could trust! In my mind I thought you couldn't be a bad thief if you stole from shops. They are insured and would get their money back. I knew Granny stole from people and that had got her into trouble with Mum. I thought, to steal from people was shameful and bad. I only broke my rule a few times when I stole money from some rich, old relatives. They had money lying all over the house, in cupboards and tins, and they never bought anything for themselves but wore the same old rags all the time. I used to visit them with Granny; it was her siblings that were loaded with all this money. I was there helping them, cleaning and tidying and also helping them in their harvest season so that I could earn some money.

Their house I helped clean was very dirty. It was very hard to scrub the floors clean enough to be able to see their original colour! My Granny's siblings never took a bath and never washed their clothes. So when I went over there with Granny, I washed all their clothes. I once boiled all their woollen underwear in the washing machine which resulted in a stack of shrunken clothes! They had suddenly changed from normal adult sizes to tiny children's sizes! This was before I learned how to use a washing machine.

When I was about the age of 11, I went with Granny to work for them for a whole week. This was the time they needed help during the harvest season, raking the fields, turning the grass to dry on the fields to make hay. I was so disappointed when Granny's brother only gave me pocket change and I felt it was very unfair. Once whilst I was scrubbing their kitchen cupboards, I suddenly saw on the top of the cupboard, bundles and bundles of 1000 Krone notes - the equivalent of many, many £100 notes, stored in little metal tins. I knew then they could have paid me much more and they didn't!

When I visited them again, when I was about 13 and working hard for them, the temptation was too much to resist. I thought they wouldn't be poor if I should take a note from one of the bundles? They didn't seem to use their money anyway and with so much money in every cupboard they wouldn't notice that one note is missing? There were hundreds of notes everywhere!

With thoughts like that, silly me felt justified to steal from them. These people were wonderful people. They loved God and they were always cheerful and happy. There was never a shortage of pop and chocolate in their house and lovely cakes. It's very sad to say that I didn't feel bad about stealing from them. I felt justified because I thought this was not money I would just go and spend on "stuff." I would not spend one bit of it yet, but I would put it in my bank to save!

With that money I was going to save for my planned escape and I started to plan when I was 13 years old. I wanted to move far away from home and I knew I needed savings, so that I could rent a room somewhere and get a job. I stole money from them three times, 1000 Kroner each time. I estimated I would have enough money to move away when I included the money I knew I would get at my confirmation celebration, when I turned 15. I was never found out stealing from those people and the sad thing

was I never had a bad conscience about stealing from them. In
my mind I just thought, with all these bundles of hundreds of
1000 Kroner notes, they would never notice any of them missing
and they would never run out of money either!

*****

Granny and Granddad came to stay at the farm again one time,
right after Christmas. Granddad had longed to come home. On
one cold February day, Granny came running from the bedroom
into her kitchen shouting, "We need to get a doctor for Granddad,
he is throwing up blood." An ambulance came and took Granddad
to the hospital sixty five miles away and they operated on his
stomach. He was away for a week. The doctors opened him up
and then stitched him back up again, saying he had cancer and
it had spread too far for them to do anything. Granddad came
home for good after that; he wanted to come home to die. I was
a permanent resident in my grandparent's bedroom, where I
watched Granddad deteriorate every day. Some days he was as
I always remembered him, but other days he was not able to eat
or drink.

When he was well enough, he spent some weekends at Sara's
house and on the 11th of June 1978, we celebrated Granddad's 84th
birthday at her house. Afterwards he went back to the farm and
his health worsened very quickly from then on. I never thought
in a million years that Granddad would die. He had lived forever
and I could not comprehend a life without him. By the end of
August he became so sick that Granny could not look after him
and they took him into a small hospital. I went to see him at the
weekend. He was placed in a lovely bright room by himself where

there was one picture on the wall opposite his bed. There was one chair, each side of the bed and I sat down by him and said, "Hey, Granddad, when are you coming home? I miss you, I want you to come home." I sat down by his bedside looking at his very old face, which had become so much thinner since the last time I saw him. Granddad stretched out his old wrinkly hand, where the veins were very thick, and his crooked fingers were now like thin, hard sticks. Shaking, he stretched forth his hand and grabbed my hand firmly. "Laila, my little bird," he said, "you must look after yourself, you must be careful. Don't let them get to you. Listen, you must stay strong. You must live, survive, and grow up to be strong." All the family came to see him and I was told later that he had held their hands, too, and asked each of them to promise to look after his little "bird." He said he couldn't believe that I would ever grow up. He was worried I would not make it.

On the 26th of September 1978, Granddad passed away, after being sick for only eight months. I was devastated and missed him so much. This was my first experience at the age of 12 of losing someone close to me. The funeral was surreal to me and I just clung onto Granny during the whole ceremony. After Granddad's death Granny never came back to stay at the farm. From then on it was just Tally and me.

I was so happy when Tally started having puppies. She gave birth several times to many litters of puppies. We tried to give them away to people, but they weren't very interested. Some took the puppies but we were always left with a few. When the puppies were about three months old they all suddenly disappeared! Dad had secretly got rid of the puppies. He took the little dogs and smashed their heads with a hammer so that they were killed instantly, then threw them in the manure basement of the barn. In those days most farmers didn't call for vets to put down any pets, they were used to doing the slaughtering themselves.

When spring time came and it was time to open up the manure basement of the barn to spread the muck on the fields for fertilizer, to my horror I saw the dried out skins of those dead little puppies, a sight a child would never forget. But thankfully one time Dad decided to keep one of the male puppies who we called Ben. I think I was about11 ½ years old when Ben was born. I loved him, but not as much as I loved Tally. We had been through so much, she was my true friend. It was fun, though, to have two dogs. I was so proud of Tally, that she had a baby. Ben soon grew big and then I had both of them to keep me warm on the floor under the kitchen table.

One day late in the autumn, when I was twelve and a half years old and following my Granddad's death, the teachers informed us that there would be a folk dance course held once a month after school for the next term. Anyone could attend and it was free of charge. The only problem was I lived so far away from school, around seven miles, and the course would not finish until 7:30 pm. In the country side in Norway you will only find three buses a day, 8 am, 2 pm and the last bus at 6 pm. I was devastated. I really wanted to attend this course and learn the very popular folkdances, so I decided to join and hope Mum or Dad would pick me up. I knew they always drove Ted for his football practise and now it was my turn to be picked up from something.

I stayed behind after school and waited for the practice. It was great fun and I loved it. After the first evening, I went to a friend's house and used their telephone to ring Mum and Dad to pick me up. Mum said there was no way in the world they would pick me up. "Make your own way home, you should not have attended this course," then she hung up. There was nothing I could do, but start to walk the long way home trying to hitch a ride, hoping a car would stop. I knew from experience that it was not easy to get a lift in the evenings. When I had walked about half way home, up the steep hills in the mountainside, I finally got lucky and a car picked me up.

When I got home I went into the kitchen where the lights were switched off and I was expecting Tally to come running to greet me, but it was quiet! It was really late and Mum and Dad had gone to bed. I went into the bathroom, cleaned my teeth, and went straight to bed. The next morning it was time for school again. Dad shouted from downstairs to get me up and I pulled myself involuntarily and very sleepily out of bed to get ready for school. I walked through the kitchen door as always and I was waiting for Tally to come jumping at me wagging her tail, but she was nowhere to be seen.

Ben was lying on his mat and wagged his tail as I walked towards him. I shouted Tally's name, "Where are you, Tally"? Looking out of the window to see if she was outside, my heart started beating faster when I could not see her anywhere. A terrible feeling came over me. I looked at Dad and asked him where Tally was, because she had never been gone before. She was only six years old. Dad was standing by the kitchen sink running the water and he just glanced towards me saying, "We had a sick sheep last night and I needed to call the vet to have the sheep seen to. I took the opportunity to get rid of Tally. We are sick and tired of Tally always having those puppies, so I had the vet put her down. Tally is dead, she didn't feel a thing. She just went to sleep when the vet gave her a shot with a poison injection. Why do you think we kept Ben, a male dog that can't get puppies?"

A knife pierced my heart. My mind was spinning, it can't be true! Not Tally, not Tally, she's got to be here somewhere! I screamed, "No you can't do that, you don't understand, she is my friend, you can't kill my friend, she is my only true friend, she can't be dead, you are a murderer, where is she, I want to go to her, I want my friend, I want to see for myself, you are just lying. Where is she?"

"Oh," Dad said, "The vet took her in a black bin bag. He is chucking her on the rubbish tip for me today where she will be burned."

I screamed in horror. "My friend burned? My friend, she was my friend and you have killed her. You have even taken her body away from me so I can't bury her, I don't even have a grave to go to. I hate you, I hate you." I ran out the door crying my eyes out and I caught the bus that took me to school.

For many days it was impossible not to cry in school and when one of the girls I had played with asked why I was crying, I told her and she giggled, saying that it was just a dog, nothing to get so upset about. I knew she couldn't possibly understand what Tally meant to me. She didn't know about the situation at home, so I didn't even try to explain. Walking into the house with Tally not there was like walking into a house made of ice. It felt cold, that is the only way I can describe it.

I don't know how many days I cried after Tally's death, but every night my pillow was wet with tears. I felt it was almost worse to lose Tally than when my Granddad died, because she was all I had left. Though we still had another dog, I didn't have that same bond with Ben. I had known Tally since I was 6 years old and it was just her and me all the time. Ben was only one year old and he had a different temperament to Tally. Tally was just nice and calm and I felt she actually understood everything I was saying to her. I believed she knew everything about me. My emotions were all mixed up with sorrow and grief. In just in a few months I had lost my dear Granddad and now it was Tally. It was more than I felt I could bear.

There was a new feeling growing inside my heart, an intense, growing hatred for Dad. It increased every day. I started to store up great anger, hurt, and bitterness on the inside. I was determined I was going to leave home as soon I turned 16 and finished school and decided then I would never come back.

Chapter 18

READY TO KILL

One evening not too long after Tally's death, Mum and Dad started to drink again. I sat by the kitchen table doing some drawings. I used to love to draw and I could work at one drawing for many days before I was finally happy with it. Granddad had told me to practise, and then I would get good at it. Once I was finished and was happy with my art, I gathered my stuff to go upstairs. Mum and Dad had started to get loud, so I thought to myself I'd better disappear. When I walked past the doorway in the kitchen by our living room, Dad spotted me and shouted as he always did when he was drunk, "You, f***ing bastard, what in the hell are you doing in my house, haven't you gone to Nicky's house yet? You have no right to be here, what in the hell are you doing here then, get the f*** out of here, you are a whore child nothing but a whore child, get the f*** out of my sight. Go over to Nicky's farm where you belong."

I stood by the cutting board in the kitchen staring at my Dad with a hatred I cannot describe in words. All I felt was spite and intense hatred while I shouted, "I hate you, I hate you. I would never want a father like you, I'd rather have any other dad but you, Nicky is fine by me. I don't want you as my Dad if that is what you think. Who do you think you are? Do you really think I would want you? Oh, no, I don't want a f***ing devil as a Dad."

Dad jumped to his feet and stood wobbling while he was pointing at me with eyes clenched in rage shouting, "Whore child, wait till I get my hands on you, I will make mincemeat out of you. I'll beat you up so bad you won't be able to walk ever again, and I will send you away to an orphanage, where bastards belong." He took one step towards me, when I turned around and grabbed a huge butcher's knife, screaming at him, "If you get so much as one inch nearer me, I will kill you, I will kill you, you f***ing bastard of a devil." I pointed the huge sharp knife straight at him with great determination. I know I would have stabbed him in the stomach if he had approached me that night.

I pictured when he would get up from his chair and walk towards me and I saw how I could kill him. I knew he was so drunk that I would be faster than him. I would be able to plunge the knife in him before he could grab me. In my mind I saw a fast forward of my life, with me stabbing Dad to death, blood everywhere, and jail for life, but I didn't care. I wanted that man dead. I hated him so much I would gladly go to jail to just get rid of him and never see him again. I felt any price was worth it.

Years later when I thought about this episode, I was so glad Dad sat down and just grabbed another beer, not continuing his abuse and not approaching me holding that knife. My life would have been totally different today. I was only about 12 ½ years old but my heart had turned into a cold, hard stone, and I knew that I was capable of killing.

The few things that had given me joy faded more and more, as I sank deeper and deeper into a dark well of "nothingness."

In the end, all I could feel was endless pain. I felt like I just existed. The pain got so bad that I forgot that there had ever been any glints of lights at all in my childhood. I spent 27 years of my life not remembering any good things that had happened to me. All I remembered was pain, and all I was doing was hurting all the time.

Chapter 19

THE TRIP ON THE SHIP

During the summer holidays in 1978, I was allowed to take the two day long journey myself on the ship to visit Nan and Auntie Wilma. This was only two years after my first trip on the ship when Mum left Dad. We always had long school holidays, about eight weeks. The school would finish around the 18th of June and we would be back by mid August. So it was a long holiday away from home.

I remember this first time alone on the ship. Dad had bought me a ticket with a cabin below deck that I shared with two old ladies. I nagged Mum and Dad to give me some spending money for my holiday, and to my surprise, they gave me a 100 kroner note (£10). Mum said I had to pay for the taxi with the money she gave me, from the dock to Nan's house, when I arrived there on Monday morning. The money had to last me for my whole two months while I stayed at my Nan's. I departed on Saturday at noon and arrived Monday morning at 4 am.

Mum and Dad drove me the 90 miles to the city where the ship departed from, and made sure I got on board. I was excited to go on the ship, but I found it strange that although Mum never said much or showed any emotions, each summer when she saw me off and said goodbye, she quickly bent down to give me a fast hug. I saw she was struggling to hold back her tears, and I was not used to see her even start to cry unless she was drunk. It was so awful to see her like that, I didn't know what to do. I didn't understand where her emotions came from. I never thought she cared, why did she almost cry, was there any sense in her of wanting me at all? I had come to terms with the fact that Ted was her favourite kid since she had let him beat me up all the time and she had never interfered with what he had done to me.

The excitement over travelling and being away for the summer was replaced with a kind of despair. I felt awfully sorry for Mum because I didn't want her to be sad. I also felt a sense of grief that I didn't really know Mum at all and she didn't know me either. I was desperately longing to have a Mum. I was longing for a relationship with her. I could not remember ever having been cuddled by her, or ever snuggling up safely on her lap just being her little girl, where she would wipe away my tears, and where I could feel safe and away from all the pain that was building up inside me.

I never remember if she brushed my hair or gave me plaster on places I would be bleeding, either after I had fallen or Ted's biting or scratching me. She never gave me any advice on what I needed to be careful of in life or asked me questions about what education to do when I finished school. I never remember having an ordinary conversation with her, like how has your day been, are you okay, what are your dreams, and so on.

There is one thing I do remember Mum did for me when I asked her and it meant a great deal to me. There was a very popular book that every schoolgirl loved to own called a memory book. Granny had given me one, a lovely red memory book, for Christmas. It was lent to our friends for them to write a short poem or rhymes to remember them by for the future. Whenever you chose someone to write in your book, they would take it home and write in their prettiest handwriting. It was always a great competition to write the heading in the most fancy and artistic way, starting with: "Memory for Laila". They could add different colouring and whatever they wanted you to remember them by, the only rule was to use only one page each, and they could start to write wherever they wanted in the book. It was very important to get the most popular pupils in school to write in your book. We even let our favourite teachers write poems and rhymes in it too.

One day I asked my Mum if she would write something for me in my book. She chose the very last page in my book to write. She wrote me a verse of an old hymn called "Alltid Freidig Når du Går." The hymn translates something like this:

"Always be courageous on the paths of life,
on the paths that only God can know,
and stay courageous right to the very end."

She also made a beautiful drawing of a pretty woman walking on a long road carrying a suitcase. I used to pick up my memory book and admire the beautiful drawing, thinking that Mum had made a drawing of me in the future. When I became an adult, this would be me off to somewhere, with my suitcase, travelling around the world far away from everything.

I was so proud of the drawing, because it was something my Mum had done for me. I clung to anything that might suggest she cared for me. Though I didn't understand the words in the hymn back then, it made me feel that I was going to be safe in the future, no matter where I was headed. I often nagged Mum to teach me how to draw like she did. She said she had forgotten how to do drawings and she didn't have time anyway, but I had already made a decision that I would learn to draw as well as that.

I brought this memory book with me on the boat, because it was a very important book to have with you at all times, with memories from loads of people. I had packed my memory book in my bag and stored it tightly under the berth in the cabin. I could not wait to run downstairs to my cabin to find my memory book and look up the last page reading through the memory Mum had written to me months before. I really missed her when I saw how sad she was when I boarded the ship. I crawled up into my berth and switched the tiny reading light on whilst I was reading the hymn Mum had written to me, admiring the drawing with the beautiful woman carrying her suitcase, walking on a small road with bends and turns till it disappeared out of the top of the page of the book. I felt tears rolling down my cheeks as I shut the memory book and hugged it tight to my chest.

The boat departed and would dock at many places before I reached my destination. There was nothing much to do on the ship except wait and take in the beautiful landscape along the amazing Norwegian coastline. With the sun not setting at all at night, it was quite an awesome sight. The further north you go, the shape of the mountains get rounder but they still stand strong and tall, although they are not rugged like in the west. Mountains towards the North have a blue glaze during the daytime, but towards the evening, when the sun hits their tops, they stand like glowing red candles. Even as a kid I never got tired of enjoying the beautiful voyage to the North of Norway.

I wanted to explore the whole of the ship so I ran around

everywhere until I finally got to the top deck outside. There were the two American ladies that were sharing my tiny cabin. They were amazed that I was travelling alone and asked how old I was. I said have a guess, and they both guessed nine. I knew I was small, but I didn't like to look like a 9 year old when I was well past 12. I had started to learn English in school the year before and I loved it and had studied a lot, so I spoke all I could to practise my English with them. They were both school teachers and they were very impressed I was able to speak so well.

I saw the two ladies later on the deck feeding the seagulls that were following the ship in big flocks. The ladies offered me some of the bread, so that I could have a go too. I stretched my hand out as far as I could, and lo and behold a huge seagull aimed for my hand and won the race among the other birds, snatching the piece out of my hand. I wanted to get a proper feed to them so I ran off to a place where I thought no one could see me. I decided to climb outside the rail on the ship. I held on to the rail with one arm as I leaned over, stretching my arm as far as I could for the seagulls to pick some food from my hand. With the sea gushing against the boat beneath me I felt I was suspended between heaven and earth.

Loads of birds flew in my direction. The wind was blowing and I almost felt like a bird myself, like I was flying together with the seagulls. I felt so free and that I could fly wherever I wanted. I had dreamed of being a bird since I was very little, so this felt wonderful. The birds were chasing each other to get a bread crust, and one of them took a wrong aim and snatched my finger instead of the bread. My daydream was cut short by the seagull biting my finger and then someone on the ship saw what I was doing and shouted to me to get away from there. They shouted that no one was allowed to go outside the rails because it was dangerous. I could fall in the water and drown. I was so used to climbing high up and running around on the narrow planks in our barn that I didn't think it was worse to climb outside the rail of the ship. I was not afraid of heights at all. I just found it exciting and I felt very brave that I dared to do it. It was all worth it for the wonderful feeling of being a bird myself.

I had brought my school backpack and a little bag containing the few clothes I owned, one pair of denim trousers, one pair of light pink trousers that Mum had made, that were torn, some underwear, a few pairs of socks, some sweaters and a couple of t-shirts. In the backpack I had also packed some apples, a couple of oranges, bananas, one bag of crisps, one chocolate and one litre of pop. Mum had told me to take sandwiches with me, but I was stubborn and refused. I couldn't chew her bread. It got stuck in my throat, and the taste was awful. Not only was it burnt like charcoal on the top and bottom and often raw inside, but it was also very salty. At school I had gotten used to not eating much food at all. I lived on sweets that I used to steal from the shop, or sometimes a day old Danish pastry that they sold very cheaply at the local bakery.

I persuaded Mum to stop at the shop to buy candies as an excuse, saying I needed something to eat on the two day journey. By Saturday evening I had eaten most of my fruit, and had just a few crisps left. Now I was starving for proper food. I had not eaten any breakfast in the morning before we left for the city; I never managed to eat breakfast. I was used to having dinner at home and I had not eaten dinner. I regretted not listening to Mum when she told me to pack sandwiches. I was so hungry I would have eaten anything, even her raw, salted bread.

I walked around the ship and I had an idea to go to the restaurant and see if I could buy some food there. I only had 100 krone (£10) to last me the whole summer and I didn't want to spend it on food, but I became so hungry that I thought I could at least check. I looked at the desk with open sandwiches, and there was a thin single slice of bread with pate on for 11 krone (£1) - in 1978 it was a fortune even then. I was so hungry that I bought the one slice, and it did not do much for me. I was still hungry, but at least it filled the gap, and I did not go to bed starving. After listening to the noise of the ship's engine for a long time, and the sound of the waves splashing through the hull, I fell asleep the first night.

Sunday came and I got up and ran around like the day before and by noon I was really hungry again. I could smell the lovely aroma of dinner. I passed the restaurant and saw it was full of passengers enjoying their food. Of course there was no way for me to afford to pay 45 krone (£4.50) for a portion of sausage and mash. I just stood on the outside deck and looked through the window of the restaurant watching everyone eat. Suddenly I saw the two American ladies that were sharing my cabin. They waved at me to come in. Maybe they had seen me drooling with longing and that was the reason they invited me in.

I ran into the restaurant and was so happy to see them because I had taken a great liking to the old ladies. The day before the old ladies kept asking me in the cabin if I was hungry and if I had food; I had said I have loads of stuff. But now they obviously had seen that I was hungry, and they invited me to dine with them. I was over the moon when I dived into the best sausage and mash I had ever eaten. I had no table manners at all and I just gulped down the food as fast as I could, followed with a burp here and there, and I also spoke with my mouth full. The two old ladies looked at each other with a small smile on their faces while they finished consuming their own meal. The women asked me lots of questions about what type of food Mum had given to me. I was a bit embarrassed when I told them the truth. I said Mum nagged me to bring food but I didn't want to, and it was my own fault not listening to Mum. I realized how stupid I had been and I regretted not listening to Mum at all. I did learn a great lesson that year, because I never went on the ship again without bringing sandwiches with me.

I was so happy to get to know these two old ladies; I became the centre of their attention and loved it as they took photos of me lining up with each of them. While we were strolling out on deck, the captain of the ship was also taking a stroll to get some fresh air. The ladies asked kindly if the captain would pose together with me, so they could take a photograph. We even exchanged addresses and became pen friends. They sent me the pictures they had taken and the next Christmas they even sent me a gift, a beautiful silver necklace with an L on, which I still have today.

Chapter 20

MY FIRST SUMMER ALONE
AT NAN'S

I arrived at my destination up North at 4 am on Monday. Mum had told me there would be a taxi waiting for me when the ship arrived; she had told Nan to book one for me. I was the only passenger that came off the ship at that dock. I came off the ship and saw no taxi there. I waited for quite a while before I figured out that I must find where the taxis are, because it was too far to walk the few miles to Nan's house uphill with my bags. But before I went off to find my lift, the taxi suddenly came and stopped in front of me. The taxi driver apologised for the delay and said the ship had arrived early. It took only seven minutes to drive to Nan's house, and it cost me 30 krone (£ 3) for the fare to get there. I now only had 60 krone (£ 6) to last me almost two months.

Nan gave me a lovely little bedroom upstairs. It had only room for a bed and a small night table, a chair and a tiny cupboard in the corner to put away my clothes, but it was so cosy, I loved it. The first few nights I struggled to fall asleep, the sun was shining as bright as day in the middle of the night. The famous midnight sun kept me awake. I asked Nan for a solution and she gave me a blanket to cover the window so that I could fall asleep more easily. The first two days I was not allowed to leave Nan's house at all. I had to sit and listen carefully to all her stories of all that she had been through, interrupted with her shouting at the voices she was hearing in the walls telling them to f***ing shut up. She thought the devil and spies had occupied her house, and that they spoke through microphones that were fixed inside the walls, with wiring all over her house.

At first when she shouted, I thought it was me she shouted at, so I jumped off my chair in fright, but I soon got used to the fact that it wasn't me she was on to, it was the voices she was hearing. In the beginning I even tried to convince her that I could not hear any voices, that they were not there. Then she went really mad and thought I was in on the plot and that I had been sent by agents to come and spy on her before poisoning her. For a while she was convinced that I was working with the enemy to make her ill, and to make her go insane from all the torture she felt surrounding her.

For the next couple of days I had to play card games with her at the kitchen table, which was very boring, because she went bananas if I won. She then changed the rules for her to win. She said if I had won one round I had to let her win the next round, that was only fair, and I of course just had to abide by her rules. There was no way I could cross Nan, she was too strict for that. She had a very sharp voice and I remember finding her eyes very scary. They were sunk deep into her head with dark shadows underneath. She stared from those sockets with a strange wildness that scared me; I guess it was the madness I could pick up in her eyes.

In the evening she dolled herself up to watch television. She said I had to sit really nice and not say any bad words in front of the telly. My language had become very bad by this age, I was swearing worse than the workers at the docks. Nan said I must not swear when the TV was on because the people in the TV could see us. She only told me off when I was swearing when the TV was on; she didn't make any remarks when I swore badly during our card games or other times when I decided to swear. Swearing had become a big part of my language by now, very often there were more swear words in my sentences than normal words. But Nan was not exactly nice in her own language; I do remember I picked up a few swear words that I had never heard before from her.

Once the twins (my cousins) came for a sleepover and we all tried to convince Nan that people could not see us from inside the TV. The twins ran in front of the telly and mooned their bums laughing their head off; Nan went bright red with embarrassment, and shouted, "What on earth would the people think of me now," while she could not stop giggling herself. Even in spite of all this, I used to think this is much better than being home.

Finally after two days of being stuck in the house, I begged Nan to go out and see if I could find some friends. But I could never think of leaving the house before I had done all the dishes and wiped and washed the floors. It took many hours to do the work, because I had never done housework before and she stood over me instructing every move I made to make sure I did a proper job and everything was up to her standard. I hated her for forcing me to do housework, but years later when I was older and had my own place, I was relieved that I had already learned how to do some things. It really helped me when I moved away from home and only then was I thankful that she had taught me, even though her methods were crazy. I learned how to make a home nice, clean, and tidy.

Once all the chores were done, I went off into the streets and had a great time. There were lots of girls playing in different parts of the long main street. But I was so anxious about all the money the trip had cost me so far, that the following day after dinner, I sat at Nan's kitchen table counting the money I had left. Nan's eyes became round and big, as if they were about to pop out of her head. She asked me what is that, had I been in her handbag and stolen money from her or what. I told her Mum had given me some pocket money to have the whole summer and I wanted to find out what was left. She became very funny and almost angry, and she said," Don't think you can just come here and live off me, do you know how expensive the milk is now? Its 1.90 krone per litre (19 pence) and you drink me out of my house. From now on you have to buy your own milk, that's for sure. You've got your own money and it will teach you that things costs, nothing is for free." I could not believe my own ears. Nan wanted me to buy my own milk! I was getting so worried and thinking how on earth I was going to make my money last when I also have to spend it on milk.

A few days later the twins Robert and Richard (age 8) and the younger brother Rick (age 6) came again to Nan's for a visit. Nan always had boxes of ice cream cones in her chest freezer and she wanted to give the kids a treat. She came back with four ice creams and we all smiled from ear to ear. Nan gave one each to the twins and one for Rick and one for herself. I asked Nan, "Where is my ice cream, can't I have one too?" "No way," she said, "are you having any of my ice creams. You have your own money so don't think you can have what I have bought with my money. Look at your cousins. They have no money at all and they are so skinny and deserve a treat."

I was so disappointed. I thought to myself, "Granny at home would never have done anything like that, she always gave all the kids the same." I was trying to figure out why I could not have an ice cream too. "I am only at Nan's once a year. The twins are here all year around and get ice creams and treats all the time, and now Nan doesn't want to give any to me because I have a little pocket money?" Nan never gave me any ice creams. Every time she just let me watch them all eat, followed by words like, "You go and buy your own. Don't think you can have any of mine."

Auntie Wilma told me later that Nan could never stand anyone having money beside her; she got so jealous even if you had a few coins that she became cruel to whoever she knew had money. It seemed as though Nan could not rest knowing I had some money.

A few days later I had to sweep all the dog's hair from the kitchen floor, then Nan gave me a bucket of boiling water and a pair of gloves and commanded me to clean the floor. Her kitchen was very small and awkward to clean, and I still didn't know how to do housework properly. With the long handle of her mop it was inevitable to bump into the work units around the kitchen. The worktops were fitted in an L shape and there was a very small kitchen table by the window blocking the way of getting around in just one sweep, so I had to move around all the time. Nan insisted I swilled up the mop just after one wipe, and I had to change the water many times till the water had no colour; she wanted the water to be as clear as from the tap before she let me clean another spot. In the opposite corner of the room was her cooker, and beside the cooker a small worktop, where she used to place her favourite china saucer and her coffee cup ready for her afternoon coffee.

I had almost finished my chores when the handle of the mop fell out of my hand and swept her cup off the worktop where it crashed on the floor in pieces. Nan went ballistic. It was her special cup, one of those you give as a present for Mother's Day. This one had beautiful double jointed writing saying "Grandmother" on the front and a lovely pink rose on the other side. She yelled and screamed what a hopeless kid I was, and how evil I was to smash her cup, and she said she knew I did it on purpose. I better go to town the next day to buy her a new one or else she would send me home. Buying her a new cup was going to teach me a lesson to take better care of other people's things.

Of course I had no choice; the last thing I wanted was to go home. I had to do as she told me. I walked around everywhere and the cheapest cup I could find cost 25 krone (£ 2.50) I knew I would soon be broke the way I was losing money. A few days later I experienced more embarrassment when Nan sent me to the local shop to pick up a few things for her. I also had to buy milk for myself. When I came to the till to pay, I had two separate lots, one lot for Nan with her money, and the milk for myself with my money. The lady at the shop knew Nan well. She was very nosy and she asked me loads of questions whilst shaking her head, saying what a cruel woman Nan was, that she could not even spare some milk for her grandchild who was visiting her only once a year. I didn't know what to say to the lady at all. This was something I just had to accept. I had to buy my own milk at Nan's every summer I visited her from then on.

Chapter 21

NAN'S PARTIES

Very often drunkards came to visit Nan. She made her own wine; her brewery was in her bathroom and I remember the distinct smell in that room. She boiled loads of red apples and rhubarb with sugar, and added raisins and other fruits too. Once everything had been brought to the boil, she added the yeast and poured it into ten litres buckets where she left the ingredients to ferment for several weeks, before she poured it into bottles and stored them away to mature. Nan was famous for her wine. Everyone called her "the mad wine woman on the hill", which was an exact description of Nan! As I mentioned before, it was impossible to buy alcohol on Saturday and Sunday in Norway, so when the local guys had hangovers after binge drinking, they went to Nan to buy their "medicine" to prevent them from getting sober—that's when the hangover kicks in, they said.

Normally, they just came to buy one bottle of wine from her, but she had ulterior motives. She was crazy about men and she always invited them in so she could sell them more bottles. She let them try the wine and have a drink with her. Then it was a done deal; of course the men started to drink, and the party was on. Nan would get all dolled up for the weekends, putting on her best clothes, and her bright red lipstick, with her red plastic pearls and matching earrings and bracelet.

Sometimes Nan even tricked the young lads into bed with her after getting them so smashed they didn't know where they were or what they were doing. They only realized the next morning what they had done, and they could be seen running out of Nan's house with tears in their eyes. Nan loved the stream of people that came to her house during the weekends. She used to say to me, "I tell the men, if they want 'some,' they can have 'some,' but I make sure to send them to the bathroom first to wash, because I can't stand having sex with a smelly man. You know most never wash and are very dirty. I sometimes get put off how dirty they are and then have to satisfy myself alone. You know, I become so lustful at times, I have to use other methods." I tried not to listen to Nan when she went into the dirty mood of just talking filth. I always felt disgusted, with my stomach turning, and I felt totally sick hearing my own old Nan talking about her so called "sex life" which she described to me in detail.

I remember when Nan had a lover from Finland. His name was Yrjan. He was a funny guy. He was quite tall, medium build with black hair combed back, and he had big black eyebrows and a huge smile stuck on a wrinkly face. He didn't know a single word in Norwegian and Nan didn't know a word of Finnish. Nan was shouting at him all the time about all the spies who were speaking to her through the walls and how there was a plot to kill her, but Yrjan didn't have a clue what she was on about. He just laughed all the time when Nan was shouting, shaking his head and pointing to the bottle, indicating he wanted more wine.

I had just started to learn English the year before, and now I wanted to learn some Finnish because I was fascinated with new languages. I picked up a few words and I can still remember them today. When Yrjan was there, I always made sure not to go out; I had learned he would give me money. When he got very drunk he emptied his pockets of change and gave it to me. I quickly hid the money so Nan didn't see it. Sometimes there could be as much as 40-50 kr (£4-5) which was well needed. I quickly found out that this was an easy way to get money.

One day I sat in the kitchen together with Nan and Yrjan. They were both drinking, and I was listening to them trying to communicate whilst laughing my head off. Nan had decided that she wanted to be generous to me this day and was showing off to her lover what a wonderful Nan she was. Nan poured me a glass of red pop, which was called fairytale pop. I used to love that pop. I had just finished my glass of pop when Yrjan started to fill my glass with red wine without Nan seeing it; he put his finger to his mouth indicating for me to not say anything to Nan while the well- known Yrjan smile covered his face. I thought this could be fun, I get to drink wine too. I just poured the wine down in one go, making sure Nan wouldn't see what I was doing. Then Yrjan poured me another one. Apparently that is how they drink in Finland, I thought; they don't mess about.

I had at least four cups of wine within one hour. Then out of nowhere I started to feel very weird and dizzy. I felt my stomach turn and I thought I was going to be sick. I got up to go to the toilet and I staggered across the floor. Nan screamed out, "What is the matter with you? My God, you are as drunk as a skunk! How on earth did you get drunk?" I just made it to the toilet before I threw up. Nan ran after me and by now she was laughing her head off over how drunk I was. She laughed and bent over and crossed her legs and laughed some more before she wet herself.

She loved playing doctor so she ran into the kitchen and found her box of medicine in the cupboard. She picked up an Alka-Seltzer that she dissolved in water and commanded me to drink. She was laughing all the time while I was mourning how sick I felt. The ceiling was spinning and everything went around and around. In the end I could not resist laughing myself. I was only 12 ½ years old and drunk for the first time, in the great care of my Nan.

*****

After a few weeks I made more and more friends up north, but they began to notice that I was wearing the same clothes all the time. They asked me if I was going to change my jeans soon. "Why you are wearing the same ones?" They bombarded me with questions. I didn't dare to tell them I had no other trousers. The only other trousers I had were split up the seams and falling apart, with big holes down the inside of the legs. They were home made, and were worn out. I always put up a tough front, so I just said, "I like these and that's that. They are Levis." I didn't say I had inherited these jeans from my cousin Ken, he had grown out of them and it was the only real jeans I had.

I had only worn home-sewn clothes, but now I was becoming more aware that everyone had denim jeans, and the other mums didn't make clothes. I didn't want to get bullied for the old fashioned clothes and I was happy that I at least had one pair. I had already started to steal chocolate, but I didn't have the courage to steal clothes for a couple more years after that.

Eventually some of my new friends, the kids I found in the streets also started to bully me and say that I was dirty. I was very hurt because I thought I was clean. Nan made me wash my face and hands and down below every evening before I went to bed. She had given me a flannel for the face and a flannel for down below. She showed me how to wash myself by stripping herself naked in front of me and she washed herself first while I was looking at her. Then she stood by my side making sure I followed the same procedures she did, face first, then other parts after.

I was really embarrassed by the kids calling me dirty and now I started to notice that my clothes were dirty after one month and I also realised that I had not taken a proper bath either. Nan didn't have a shower, just a bath tub. I asked Nan if I could please take a bath. She strictly refused, and said I had to wait till she was taking her bath and I could go into the water after she was finished. After a few days finally Nan decided to take a bath, but before she climbed into the bath tub she washed her private parts by the sink. She said it is very unhygienic to climb into the bathtub without washing your private parts first.

Nan enjoyed herself for one hour in the bath. I had to help her scrub her back and finally it was my turn to climb in. She added more hot water for me, and it was so lovely with the bubbles that appeared when she added the hot water and the smell of pine bubbles was all over me. The bubbles soon went out and the water changed colour to very dark brown. Nan came into the bathroom after a few minutes to check on me and I saw she got the shivers when she saw how dirty the water was.

"My God," she yelled, "Why are you so dirty? My God, you have been wandering around my house like a dirt bag! Let me look at your clothes." They were, of course, filthy, and after my

well needed clean up, she got out a bucket and filled it with soap
and water and I had to wash my clothes at her kitchen sink. There
was no way she was going to wash my clothes; I had to learn
she said. I was getting older and this was the way of life. I had
to scrub the clothes till they were clean, and rinse them in cold
water till there was not so much as a bubble or a slight dirty
colour left. Clear water was the indication that the items were
properly cleaned.

I was never allowed to take my own bath at Nan's house; I
always had to use the water she had been in first. Later on during
my teenage years when I visited her, I became very fussy. I felt it
was disgusting and could not stand the thought of using the same
water as Nan used, even though she washed herself beforehand.
She still smelled of urine. I mostly managed to take a shower at
Wilma's house.

After six weeks, Mum and Dad arrived. They had finished
their harvest and now had two weeks off. They would never stay
sober on any of their holidays. They were binge drinking and
arguing on and off throughout the whole holiday. If they didn't
fight each other, they found someone else to fight with. It was no
problem for me, though because I stayed out of their way. I was
out most of the time, running around in the streets doing all sorts
of things.

*****

The summer came and went, and normal routine began
again in the autumn when school started. Being at Nan's for the
summer had helped stop the continuing coughs that bothered me
all the time while I was home. But arriving home I was soon back

to normal, my throat and chest were sore from all the cigarette smoke. As the climate became cooler and autumn appeared, I used to get throat infections. I was never taken to the doctor and given medicine of course, I just had to ride the illnesses through as always. I had over the years also struggled with loads of ear ache which made me cry all night with pain.

When I had pain in my throat, I used to take a mirror and check and see if my tonsils were red and the little thing that was hanging right at the back of my throat. One day while I was examining my throat in the kitchen mirror my sister Mary walked through the door. Mary was home for a short visit. She asked, "What you are doing with your mouth wide open like that?" I told her that my throat was really sore and I wanted to see if it was red, because I knew what was coming next if it was red. She said, "Let me have a look," and when I opened my mouth for her to get a good look, she gasped in shock and asked me if Mum had seen it. I said no, she never looks at my throat, and Mary said in anger, "Well, Mum needs to look at this right now."

Mary marched into the sitting room where Mum was sitting watching TV. She shouted to Mum, "Have you not seen Laila's throat?"

Mum gazed up to see what Mary wanted, and said "What are you talking about?"

"Come here and have a look at this."

Again I opened my mouth for Mum to get a look.

Mary said, "Can't you see that there is hardly any room in between the tonsil for anything to pass. I don't think you can even get a thin pencil between there."

"My tonsils have always been that big, and there has always been that little room in between them," I told her. I knew that because I had always wondered why I had those two huge bulks in the back of my throat and wondered how the food could pass.

Mary said, "If Laila doesn't get treatment for this she will not be able to pass any food through that small hole, and also if the tonsils swell up more with all the throat infections she is having she can risk choking and not getting enough air."

A few days later Mum arranged for me to see a doctor. My throat was not so sore anymore when I arrived at the clinic, but the doctor took one look at me and told Mum that my tonsils had to be removed ASAP. He would refer me to the hospital, and write a note on the referral—high priority. I was very excited! I was going to the hospital; this was going to be so cool. I had only been to the doctor once when I had broken my arm in school when I was nine years old. I don't know how many weeks I waited before I was admitted to do the surgery. But I know it had become winter because I remember that the ground was covered with snow.

The day I was due in Mum drove me the 90 miles to the hospital. It took three hours to get there. We also had to cross a fjord with a ferry. I was very excited because Mum stopped at a shop where she bought me a pair of fluffy slippers and a lovely night dress I could wear at the hospital. It was a blue night dress with picture of a pretty girl holding a bunch of flowers in her hands wearing a beautiful hat. (I have kept the nightdress to this day).

I had to arrive at the hospital without eating since the night before because they were going to put me to sleep. I don't remember much when I first woke up. All I remember is I had a lot of pain and I was unable to swallow. I was very excited when I was offered ice-cream to eat, but it was too painful to even manage to swallow that. Mum had waited for me to wake up after the anaesthetic but eventually Mum had to leave me at the hospital and drive the long journey home. Mum said she would come and pick me up in seven days and that she could not afford to take the long journey just to come and visit me at the hospital—that would be a total waste. The doctors said I had to stay in the hospital for that long before I could go home. I don't know why it was so long, but I guess in those days they did things a lot differently.

I didn't think much of Mum leaving then, but I did after. When Mum left I was all excited; it was all new and I liked it at the hospital. I didn't mind Mum leaving me for seven days, and I never expected her to bother to take the long journey to visit me either. But after one day I became very restless and emotional. I became aware of all the other kids having their mums and dads visiting them and making a big fuss over how brave they had been to have gone through with surgery. The parents brought little gifts for their children and special treats and hugged and squeezed their kids to comfort them. No one came and visited me at all, and I didn't hear from my parents for the whole week I stayed at the hospital.

Again I was filled with embarrassment and great sense of loneliness, the same feeling I'd always lived with. I was longing for a mum like the other kids had, and I wanted to be a little girl too. But luckily I was never short of a plan to deal with the hurt that I was feeling. I subconsciously decided to distract myself by exploring the other units of the hospital when the parents were around. Staying away from the ward when parents came made it easier for me not to feel so lonely, and to stand out. I thought that no one would know that I didn't have visitors. When seven days had passed, Mum finally came and picked me up and we went home to my great relief.

*****

The year passed by and I was longing more and more for the day to arrive when I could finally leave home just like I'd planned for so many years. Nothing much happened the year I was 13, just the same routine over and over again, going to school, coming home, doing homework. I spent the evenings sitting at the dining table doing drawings, watching some TV and going to bed. Of course Mum and Dad had their binge drinking seasons on and off, and the same hell broke loose in the house each time. But Ted was minding his own business, hanging out with his mates, going to parties, and off to football training. He had lost interest in making my life hell, which was a great relief. Still I didn't care anymore. All I could think of was being 16 and finishing school, so that I could leave that God-forsaken place and move as far away as possible. I thought that if I left home all my problems would go away and I would not hurt any more. I couldn't have been more wrong.

Chapter 22

BECOMING REBELLIOUS

When I turned 14 my school grades started to go down; I lost all interest in everything that had to do with school. When I came home from school I ran to my room and locked myself in, hoping nobody had seen that I had arrived. I hated it at home. I felt anxious most of the time and found it impossible to relax. I had been struggling to fall asleep for years. I normally went to bed about 12.30 pm, and there was no point to even try to go to bed earlier. I had tried it many times but I could never fall asleep. It often took me several hours to fall asleep, and when I finally did, I had horrible nightmares that haunted me throughout the night.

The moment I dropped off, I would feel like I was falling. It would make me jump and my heart would race so that I would be wide awake again, and have to start all over again to try to get to sleep. I had the same nightmares repeatedly—I was trapped in our house and there was fire all around. The whole mountainside was burning and the fire was consuming everything in its path on its way towards our house. I had repeated dreams about volcanoes popping up right outside the door with lava flows surrounding the house so I could not escape. I tried to escape by jumping on the lava crust but it cracked and bubbled red underneath me so that I had to run back to the house. I was trapped inside the house which was being consumed by flames. I used to wake up terrified and covered in sweat.

I also dreamt about the house and the barn being burnt down and I had to flee into the forest without knowing where to go, watching in horror whilst everything was burnt to the ground and thinking about the sheep in the barn that must have died painful deaths. Or I dreamt that I was being chased by a monster that I never caught a glimpse of but the monster was inches away from catching me. I woke up terrified. Then I dreamt about big hurricanes and tornadoes that were sweeping through the valley, tearing the roof off the room where I was sleeping. I dreamt I clung to my mattress hoping I would not be caught up in the tornado funnel. I woke up exhausted and found it hard to concentrate in school. I was always tired.

*****

I eventually started to find pleasure in going to the dances that were held in village halls each weekend at different villages. I made my way there by hitch hiking and trying to find a lift back home when the dance was finished. When I was older I very often didn't go home. I just went to people's places to continue to party. I started to live for the weekends where at least something was happening and I actually had fun. I was not stuck on a mountain far away from people; I discovered there was a civilisation on earth.

I was carrying a strange lump of hurt inside me that grew stronger and stronger each day. My emotions went up and down like a yoyo, probably like they often do with teenagers. But I carried an enormous amount of pain from my Dad's rejection and my Mum's lack of protection from Ted, which continued to grow inside of me, and I found that very difficult to handle.

When I was 14 I was desperate to stay different from everyone else. I knew I was different, I had been told so since I was a child and I didn't belong anywhere. I was the "whore child" and my siblings were just "half sisters and half brother." That was what I had been told over and over by Dad in his drunken rages. Granddad used to quote the saying, "You always get the truth from little children and from people who are drunk." I believed it back then, even though when Dad was sober he also probably meant it when he said that I wasn't his kid. I don't agree with that statement today—you do not get the truth from drunken people; you get their perception of what they think is true.

Most youth my age were already smoking, but I decided to stay a non smoker. Although I had started smoking at seven and inhaled for two years, I never became addicted. Luckily I had seen a programme on TV when I was nine that showed pictures of a man with a hole in his throat from smoking. He had to talk through a special microphone. At that moment I quit smoking because I didn't want to reach 50 and have a hole in my throat! I thought the other kids were fools with such a high risk of getting a hole in their throats. I was a black and white person. I was glad though that so many were smoking at that time, because I was desperate to be unlike everyone else –I wanted to do the opposite of what everyone else was doing.

I had a school identity card that I used to fake my age to be one year older than I actually was. Because of this, I was allowed at the dances where the age requirement was 15. In the early 80's out in the country, there were no discos, only dances with live bands playing. The dances would start at 9 pm and finish at 1 am. Then, whoever had been to the dance would go to different places or cabins to continue to party into the early morning hours.

The first time I drank a bottle of lager I didn't like it at all. I was given a small bottle, and I spent at least three hours trying to get it all down. I took such a long time to drink it that I didn't get drunk at all. At other parties I was offered spirit which was very strong and at those times I took big sips from the bottle and it didn't take long before I was smashed out of my head, just like I had been at Nan's a couple of years earlier. Not long after drinking I felt sick, everything was spinning and I threw up. I thought spirit was better to drink, because I got drunk very quickly without drinking a lot. I didn't like the taste of it either, but it helped me to get drunk. I didn't like to get too smashed because I didn't like it when I got sick. Therefore, I became more careful when I drank and made sure to not drink too fast.

Very soon I started to hitchhike to parties further and further away, sometimes up to 30 miles away. I wasn't old enough to buy my own alcohol but drank the drinks that other people gave me. One weekend I decided to go to a party that was about 40 miles away. I knew I could easily get there by hitchhiking, if I started early enough in the evening. I never gave much thought of how I would get home. This was so far away, though, and I wasn't sure if there would be a lift home in my direction. This time I had been invited to go with a girl called Lisa. She was 18 and she told me not to worry about how to get home, there was always a way. Though I was becoming more rebellious, had a big mouth and put on a tough face, I was just pretending. It was not the real me. I was still a very shy and insecure girl on the inside. Lisa had partied for several years and she knew how to play the game. I was so excited that I was invited by her and I could not wait for the party to begin. When I arrived at Lisa's house she offered me some alcohol and we drank to get into the party mood before we left for the dance.

I was of course under age but had my false identity card so I was allowed into the village hall without any questions. The dance floor was full and soon a boy came over and asked if I wanted to dance. In those days you always danced as a couple, boys or girls. It didn't matter who you were dancing with as long as you were on your feet and having fun.

After an hour of playing, the band took a short break and all the young people hung around outside in the warm and light summer night. Lisa went outside to walk around where the cars were parked to see if anyone could offer her alcohol. People used to sit in the parked cars and drink (not the driver). I followed her and also enjoyed the drops that were so hard to get a hold of. It didn't take long before I was not sober. After the break the music started again and people made their way back into the village hall. As soon as the band started to sing slow love songs, the boys and the girls began to snog each other on the dance floor. They were stuck like velcro to each other's mouths.

I felt a bit uneasy. I was 14 years old and I had never kissed anyone before. I didn't know how to kiss and I decided I need to find someone to practise on. Feeling a bit tipsy after the few mouthfuls of spirit I got brave and went back outside to look for a target. I thought to myself I can't find a tall boy, I won't be able to reach. I spotted a short boy I had never seen before. He was leaning on the wall of the village hall and laughing together with some friends. I ran over and said, "Hey! You are a good looking boy, and you are not too tall either, let's kiss!" I never asked his name. I was a bit tipsy and I don't remember what he said, but soon I was latched onto his lips as a baby is glued to its mother's breasts.

First our teeth crashed with a pling. I didn't know I had to open my mouth wider; it was not comfortable at all, then more shock — awful wet saliva floating all around my mouth. But that was not the worst of it; suddenly a horrible soft tongue just like jelly entered my mouth and started to circle mine. I was about to give it a miss, but I thought to myself I'd better try to concentrate so I won't throw up and maybe I will learn this once and for all. With that thought I persevered with the horrible kissing. I am sure we kissed almost non stop for about 30 minutes, and when I felt I had the hang of it I said I had to go to the toilet and I never saw him again.

At the time I was 14 ½ I decided to become partial punk. I did not want to become full on punk, just half, so I at least could be something in between. I wanted nobody to be able to put me in a box and say what type of person I was. I found dog collars with long steel nails that I painted black with shoe ink and wore around my neck. I wore chains around my arms and leatherette trousers that I bought cheap from a boy who had grown out of them. I managed to get a hold of a real motorbike jacket in black leather. I stuck all sorts of labels onto my biker's jacket and one of them said "Kiss me, I'm a rebel." I loved that. I also attached thick chrome chains from one shoulder of the jacket to the other.

I decided to wear clothes that were modern and it gave me great pleasure to easily steal all the clothes I wanted. Whenever I decided that I needed something, I would just shoplift to get it. I also stole a pair of black cowboy boots with big golden stars all over to match my bikers' jacket. I got a hold of some flowery tunics that had an oriental look with embroidery all over. I wasn't a proper punk, I wasn't a proper anything. I liked to wear the biker's jacket best but I used all sorts of clothes and different things to mix it up on purpose. One thing was sure, I didn't want people to put me in a box.

I listened to Billy Idol, Kiss, and Adam and the Ants. I loved a hard rock punk artiste called Nina Hagen from Germany. I had big posters of her in all sorts of punk outfits on my walls. But funny enough, I also loved ABBA, which was totally different from all the other pop groups. I listened to ABBA songs and had posters of them covering my bedroom walls. I also had a poster of a head of a goat with devil eyes that were boiling in a saucepan filled with blood.

It was so easy to steal and I had great fun in doing it. I distracted the shop attendants by joking with them and I was always loud, laughing and giggling, which I knew was not expected when you were meant to be unseen. I put on all of my charm and made sure I got loads of attention from everyone in the shop where I was going to perform my stunt. I did the opposite of what I thought a thief would do. I had no scruples or fear at all. I took what I wanted even if it was in front of their noses whilst laughing and giggling and telling jokes to the shopkeeper. Sadly, I never got caught, as that would probably have put a stop to my hobby.

Often after school a girlfriend and I often went out on "stealing raids" as we called them. We would sneak on to the bus before the driver got in and hide at the back of the bus on the floor. That way we travelled 26 miles for free to the village which had clothes shops. We filled our school bags with new jeans and tops till we felt satisfied. Then we hitchhiked back home or caught the last bus. It was a joy to go shop lifting and I just took whatever I wanted. I was never scared when I was stealing, I thoroughly enjoyed it. I had gone for so long without things that I wanted, and now I was able to get what I wanted.

So many new opportunities opened, and I didn't have to worry any longer about what I would do when I lived on my own, with this endless free supply from the shops. It meant I could save all the money I managed to get, to move away from home. I knew I needed to save up enough money to rent a room somewhere. I became so addicted to stealing that I never entered a shop without stealing something. I thought to myself, "If it's all free I can't just leave without at least something." I had no conscience at all in this matter. In my head I truly believed that the shops were insured and they got their money back anyway, so nobody loses out. In my opinion the insurance companies were legalised fraud anyway, so they deserved to lose their money.

Chapter 23

TURNING 15

A big tradition in the Norwegian culture is the christening of babies and confirmation of the young adults. If you are a member of the Lutheran Church of Norway, the age of 14 is the time to start the one year compulsory study at church to get confirmed the following spring. All my siblings had done it, and now it was my turn. For a whole year, our school grade went to church every Monday morning and had to study with the priest for one hour.

I didn't like it at all. The priest was very weird. When he spoke, he often threw his head back in a funny way so that I thought he would fall off his chair and land on his back on the floor. Then his eye balls would roll back in his head as he dived forwards again. All we saw were the whites of his eyes. Of course we tried to hide from him that we were laughing at the funny faces.

The study itself was boring and I didn't understand a thing he was talking about. I thought the Bible verses were the most boring thing I had ever read. I hated reading anyway, no matter what it was. The Bible reading made me hate reading even more. We were studying at the back room of the church; in English it is probably called the vestry. The room where we were studying was freezing cold, sometimes down to -2c. But we all knew we would have a big party in the spring and we would get loads of money when we got confirmed. That is why I decided to get confirmed and for no other reason. During the study we were given certain Bible verses to memorise by heart, and I found it very difficult to memorise something I couldn't understand. But I staggered through to learn them.

The spring finally came and with it the tradition of buying new clothes to be confirmed in. Although we were going to wear white gowns at the church for the ceremony, new clothes were a must. Mum went shopping in the big city in the west. Mum bought me a nice navy blue blazer and she tried to find a dress for me, but her budget was very tight. I could only have a dress for 100 kr (£10). I found a very pretty green concertina dress that reached just below my knees. It was fitted around my waist and the neck had a nice v cut, not too low. It had a lovely sewn on pattern in white cotton. The dress looked like one from the 1950s, and it looked so nice on me.

I was thinking to myself, if the dress doesn't work, I can always steal another one. When I came home I discovered the dress was so thin you could see right through it. There was no way I dared to wear that for the confirmation in case we had to take our gowns off. I was too shy to show off my body in a church because I didn't know when we were supposed to put on our white gowns. I realized I needed to dress more conservatively on that day; after all I was going to church. I only had a few days to get a non see-through dress and I made my way to the village where I used to steal all my other clothes.

I went to a very expensive shop that I had never stolen from before, but there were loads of conservative clothes there fit for the occasions. In its very expensive collection I found my target. It was a light blue dress with a rounded neck and a lovely embroidery pattern around the chest and back. The dress also had a fixed petticoat and a lovely silk belt which tied up like a ribbon at the back, and on the front was a beautiful embroidered butterfly. It cost a fortune, 476 kr (£47). I had never stolen anything that expensive before, and I felt an adrenaline rush as I performed my stunt. I had become an excellent thief by now and I had no problems at all getting that dress out of the shop unseen. The thought of the dress being so expensive gave me a kick I never had before. I felt really proud that I had gotten such an expensive dress. I thought to myself, if there is a God out there, I am sure he would love my dress too. At least I had made sure I didn't show up in church with a dress you could see through!

Finally my big day arrived, May the 24th 1981. The farm is located quite high up in the mountains, 450 meters (1500ft) above sea level. By the 24th of May the snow was still thick on the ground. Amazingly the trees were covered with small green buds which seemed to proclaim that the snow had to let go of its hold—spring is here! The procedure went well in church and I knew how to answer the two questions about the Bible verses the priest asked. The eight other candidates had no problem either, so a whole year of very boring Bible study in freezing conditions with a weird priest was finally over.

At home Mum had prepared for the party for many days. She had made all kinds of cakes and cooked a lovely dinner with my favourite dessert, prune fruit compote with cream. All my four godparents came to my party. One of my godparents was Nicky, the man that Dad claimed was my father. After dinner all the guests sat in the living room chatting with each other. I opened all the greeting cards filled with money and all the presents I had received.

I noticed out of the corner of my eye, Dad's eyes roving from Nicky to me, as if he was checking out any resemblance between us. With me being so near Nicky and my Dad comparing us, I felt anxiety rise up on the inside, like a ticking bomb about to go off. Thoughts went through my head like lightning. This was Dad's opportunity to finally get rid of me; he could just hand me over to Nicky. A knife went through my stomach; I could hear echoes of Dads drunken screams, "You whore child, get out of my sight, you are Nicky's kid, not mine."

I looked at Nicky, too, trying to figure out if he was my father. I saw his thin, blond hair, and his big red nose and large chin. His eyes were small and his head was very round. I tried to imagine him being my Dad, to see what I would feel, but I felt nothing, no connection at all. I turned my head around again and saw Dad had his mind somewhere else; he was busy speaking to one of the other guests. I was so relieved that Dad didn't do what I had feared seconds before, and my big day could continue unaffected by any trouble.

Mum made a great party for me and I had a wonderful day. Once I had opened all the envelopes I was over the moon when I counted 4300 krone (£430). I knew there needed to be no more worries over how I would get the money to leave home. I was 15 years old and confirmed, but I still had one year left before I could leave.

Chapter 24

WRONG PLACE, WRONG TIME

S pring came and went, and my annual summer holiday with Nan was soon going to be next on the list. But a few weeks before I left I had a very upsetting experience. I had partied almost every weekend for almost a year. Mum and Dad never gave me any boundaries. I used to say I was "not brought up, but dragged up." I just came and went as I pleased. I didn't even bother to say what I was doing or where I was going for the weekends. As far as I was concerned, they didn't care because they never asked me or showed any interest in my life either. The reason I believed that is that I was sometimes gone for three days, and when I returned they never asked if I was okay or where I had been. I hitchhiked everywhere and it could have easily gone wrong several times.

I particularly remember one episode when I was in real danger. It happened in the afternoon of a lovely sunny day. I had purposely missed my school bus to go home; I wanted to visit a girlfriend after school. I had no cash for the 6 o'clock bus so hitchhiking was my only way to get home. To me that was just an ordinary form of transport. After quite a while I got lucky and a big lorry stopped. It was always easy to get a lift with lorries. I guess the lorry drivers found it boring to drive alone all the time and they normally loved to have a chat with you when they picked you up.

This lorry driver was in his mid thirties, and as soon as I jumped in his lorry and he put his foot on the pedal, he started to make sexual advances. He told me I could come with him to have some fun and he would then take me to a party. The lorry driver had a walky-talky which he used to quickly phone his friend driving another lorry ahead of him, saying he had picked up a sexy young lady and was he ready for some fun. Listening to the conversation between the two men, I started to get very scared.

I thanked God in my head that I had been scared before, and I knew that in certain situations it is very important not to show that you are scared. I quickly pulled together a plan in my head and then I put on an act. I started to laugh and do the opposite of what I thought he would expect. I japed a way and boiled together a bunch of lies. I remember the conversation as clear as day.

I told him, "I would love to come with you, that would be so exciting, but you know I have such strict parents and they expect me home any minute. I missed the 6 o 'clock bus, so I had to hitchhike. I tried to phone them but the lines were busy, so my parents are probably already starting to ring around to find me. I am afraid that if I don't show up within the next hour they will call the police. They have done that before, only about seven months ago. My parents are so stupid and overprotective—I can't stand them. I can't wait to move out." I continued, "Thank God you gave me a lift so I will be home in time and not all hell will break loose. It would have been real fun to take you up on that offer, God knows I love to party, that's the only thing I live for. Maybe some other time if you are ever near where I live, you can stop by and pick me up and I'll go with you to a party then."

By now we had arrived near my house and I said he needed to let me off. I pointed to the house of the neighbouring farm and said I lived there. The guy grinned broadly, flattered that he thought I fancied him and said jokingly, "Okay, I'll let you off for now, but be ready for me next time." "Of course," I said, "I wouldn't miss a party for the world." He stopped the lorry, winked at me and let me off. As I walked down the road towards my house, my whole body was shaking. It was an absolutely terrifying experience.

*****

Only a few weeks later I went on my holiday to Nan's, taking the two day journey on the ship as I did every year. Having no boundaries since I was three and being used to come and go as I pleased, it was very irritating to stay at Nan's. I felt like I had arrived at a youth prison when she told me I had to be home by 11 pm. "11pm?" I thought. "Is the woman mad? What about next Monday, that's more like it." She didn't know I had started to party and drink; she thought I was just out with the girls in the streets. I made up lies that I was doing sleepovers at girls' houses, and she reluctantly gave in. When Nan sometimes refused to let me go and have "sleepovers", and I was not in by 11 pm, she locked me out so I would sleep outside. In the end I bought a little tent for 198 krone (£19) that I put up in her garden and I slept there one night when I came home too late. But she went more ballistic then and said she would send me home if I didn't come back at the time she set.

I knew I had to obey her, so I started to tell more lies and to tell her about the wonderful girls I had gotten to know and what proper families they came from. In fact, I had gotten to know some people in town who told me about a house where the parents were away for the summer. Parties were going on there all the time. The house had been entrusted to the 19 year old son called Kenny, but he had been away for the weekend earning money by fishing. Fishing was the normal source of income in the north of Norway, and if it was a good season, people could earn a small fortune in a short period of time.

Kenny had let a 23 year old man named Steven stay there for the weekend. Steven had "opened" the house and whoever could walk or crawl came to the so-called open house to have fun. Steven was apparently heartbroken because his girlfriend had finished with him. Steven declared he would kill himself by drinking himself to death and he would drink from morning to night till he died.

When I heard about the "open house" I told a girlfriend that it would be great if we could spend the weekend there and have fun. I swilled up a bunch of lies to Nan that I was going for a sleepover, but she didn't buy it. "If you don't come home by 11 pm tonight, you will find your suitcases on the stairs outside in the morning, and you will be sent home," she threatened. I didn't answer her. I didn't care about what she said. I left the house determined to go to this house party. I thought to myself, I will just have to sleep in the tent for the rest of the summer. I don't give a shit what she says, the woman is mad anyway. I want to have fun and that's it.

The trademark of the people up north is their humour. They have no problem making fun of absolutely nothing and it becomes hilarious. At the party there where people everywhere laughing, telling jokes, and playing loud music. I wet myself laughing—and of course all the alcohol helped everyone have great fun. The time was well past midnight and there were people snogging each other on settees in the living room and drunken people everywhere. There was complete chaos. I was only 15 years old and most of the people there were four to eight years older than me.

The parties I was used to going to back home were totally different. They were community hall dances with a lot younger people who would just kiss on the dance floor and walk outside hand in hand. I had never seen anything like this before. Since I was the new girl in town, some of the boys showed quite an interest in me, which I found flattering and surprising. I had never had attention like that before.

The heartbroken Steven started to flirt with me and challenged me to sit on his lap. He said he was so heartbroken that he was determined to drink himself to death. He said he needed someone to comfort him and, by the way, "I am a good kisser." He wanted to find out if I was a good kisser too. I had not been drinking too much yet, just feeling a little bit tipsy. I had chosen to drink beer instead of spirit. I thought Steven was an "old guy" and not exactly ugly and for a laugh I just jumped on his lap.

He instantly plunged his face into mine and started to snogg me very intensely. Soon his hands went all over me. I had never kissed anyone like that before and I started to feel uneasy and scared. I looked around and saw lots of other people doing the same thing. I calmed down a bit, thinking this is normal. Steven was 23 and I was only 15 and still a virgin, with no experience of sex, yet I knew very soon that Steven wanted more than a kiss.

There was no way I wanted to have sex with this man; kissing is one thing, but sex, no way. I had not even started to think of sleeping with anyone. I was very shy and prepared to wait, at least till I fell in love and had a proper boyfriend.

I tried to push his hands away from my breasts and wherever he was feeling me, but he had been at sea and was very strong. I was unable to prevent him from touching me everywhere. Suddenly an idea went through my head about how to get loose from him. I said I had to go to the toilet or else I would pee on him. I said I would come back, hoping he would forget by then, because he was quite drunk and I knew people then easily forget things. He let me go and I went into the hallway to find the toilet.

But before I knew it Steven had followed me into the hallway. He grabbed my arm and said, "Come on upstairs and I'll show you some things." "No way," I said. "I am not going upstairs with you; I'm not interested." At that Steven started to pull my left arm, and with my right arm I grabbed hold of the drawers of a huge chest of drawers to try to prevent him from pulling me up the stairs. The chest of drawers fell over and I couldn't hold on any longer. I fought and resisted all I could, but he was too strong.

A thousand thoughts ran through my head. My heart was racing in my chest ready to explode. I felt like I couldn't breathe; everything happened so fast, but still it felt like it was all in slow motion, like what I was experiencing was not real. The music was so loud in the house and there was so much noise from all the shouting and laughing, that when I screamed from the hallway, no one heard. He quickly pulled me like a rag doll up the stairs by one arm and threw me on the bed, before he turned around and locked the door. I don't know why I reacted as I did, and why I stopped fighting, but I just lay on the bed stiff as a corpse. I froze.

I did not even try to jump out the window. I just lay there, not daring to move, my mind racing: this man will kill me, do I have to let him do this, do I stand a chance of getting out of this.

Steven turned around after locking the door, pulled down his trousers and walked towards the bed. I was totally paralysed; I didn't fight him at all, like I had done downstairs in the hallway and when he dragged me upstairs. He pulled off my clothes and soon he was over me and preformed what he intended to do. I just shut my eyes not making a sound, but I was screaming on the inside: this is not happening, I am dreaming, what now, what can I do, I can't stop him, I can't stop him, at the same time regretting how stupid I had been sitting on his lap and kissing him. Why didn't I jump out the window when he turned around to lock the door? I felt it was my entire fault and I was the guilty one. If I had not sat on his lap, this would not have happened. What if I had not lied to Nan and came home at 11. This was all my fault.

It felt like something inside me went into a dial tone. I was present, but I was not present. It was like being in a cloud that was not real. I was not myself, this was happening to someone else. But something very real was taken from me in that moment; I had no ownership over my body any longer. It had been taken from me and I felt like I was in a bubble, cut off from the rest of the world, numb.

Once Steven finished his deed, he joked and laughed and asked if I enjoyed it as much as him. He jumped out of bed, got dressed and commanded me to stay in bed for the rest of the night. He wanted to grab some more beer and come back and have more fun. "Don't move," he said. "I'll be back soon, and we will have great fun, you and me." I was laying on my back staring at the ceiling, not even able to cry. I really wanted to cry, but I couldn't. I thought this is not real, this has not happened to me. How could he say things like that? Doesn't he know what he just did? Did he really think I wanted it?

Shivers went through my body just thinking of him coming back. As soon as he left the room I hurried and put my clothes on and ran downstairs into the living room. I felt so dirty, but there was no way I dared to take a shower, in case someone came and wanted to use the bathroom. There were no way I could go back to Nan's at this time either, as it was in the middle of the night and I knew if I was able even to wake her, she would not let me in. To sleep in the tent seemed too scary for me — what if someone found me and did the same thing to me Steven had just done? I knew I had to stay until the morning. The midnight sun was still shining and it was bright and clear as noon, even though it was almost 4 am. The living room was crowded with thick cigarette smoke and people, but many had fallen asleep, some on the floor, some on chairs, and some under tables.

I looked around and saw Steven was there. He was drinking beer and boasting to some people that he just had gotten laid. The party was still on, he said. I wanted to hit him, but I didn't dare. I tried to make myself invisible from him and mingled around, hoping he would not see me. But a chill went through me when I heard him shout, "Hey, Laila, what are you doing up? I told you to stay in bed. I told you I would be back." The presence of so many other people made me bold, and I told him to f*** off. I decided not to leave the crowd because he would not be able to force himself on me in the living room with people there.

I didn't sleep a wink all night. I sat up talking and joking to those who had not passed out, sipping a few more bottles of lager, pretending as if nothing had happened, wanting to forget all about it. In the back of my mind, though, I was thinking that it was all my fault. Even if I went to the police I thought they would not believe me. They would say it was my fault. When you are stupid enough to kiss a drunken guy, I thought the police would tell me I was asking for it.

I didn't get too drunk while I was waiting for the morning to arrive so I could go back to Nan's house. She would be mad enough that I had not obeyed her to be home at 11 pm, and I didn't want to give her more reasons by coming home drunk. Finally the morning came. I knew Nan would be up and I could walk home. I was expecting to find my suitcases on the outside steps, but I was about to witness something completely different. As if my world wasn't mad enough at this point, what happened next topped it all.

*****

I knew Nan was a racist by the way she spoke about coloured people, even though coloured people were hardly ever to be seen in this part of Norway. In those days you mostly only saw coloured people on TV. If there were a program on TV with a coloured person, Nan would shout at the TV in anger and disgust, thinking they could hear her. She would shout things like, "You niggers, you come over here and want to mix the races. You are unclean, and now you want to pollute the white race. F*** off to hell with you, blackies! I wish you would all go to hell." I argued with her a lot about her racist attitudes.

When I was walking home from the party, and neared Nan's house, I could hear a loud sharp woman's voice shouting from afar. The closer I approached I could tell it was Nan's familiar voice. I thought to myself, what on earth has happened now? Has someone finally come to put her away? But sadly that was not the case. From far down the street I saw Nan with her apron on and the head scarf she used to wear when she was doing housework. Blankets, duvets, rugs, cushions and mattresses were chucked on the outside landing of her stairs and all other sorts of things were trashed outside. She was hysterical and beating the items in rage screaming in the loudest, most penetrating voice I ever had heard.

"Now they have sent the nigger nits to our village! Everyone listen up! There are niggers nits amongst us! The f***ing niggers have now come to this country and they are spreading pests!" I was so embarrassed I didn't know what to do with myself; I hoped she would fall off the landing and break her legs as she was leaning forward beating the fabrics. I was totally drained mentally and physically after the previous night's event. And now I had to find a place in my mind to store this impression. Many neighbours heard her screams and were outside watching her "circus." In one way I was relieved she was more concerned with the nits and forgot to chuck me out of her house, but it was awful to see her gone so nuts.

What I soon learned was that the twins were visiting Nan and they had showed her the nits they had contracted at school. Auntie Wilma had strictly forbidden the twins telling Nan they had nits, because she knew Nan would go bananas. Wilma was too embarrassed herself to go to the pharmacy to get treatment for her boys, so she sent a note and money with the twins to buy it for themselves. Of course the twins had to make their way via Nan's house to show her their nits. The twins always did the opposite of what they were told, and they were quite proud they had nits because it brought them a lot of attention. They were laughing their heads off over Nan's ludicrous behaviour.

When she saw me, she yelled, "Where in the hell have you been? I have been working all morning and I am totally exhausted and about to get a heart attack. You should have been here and helped me. If I die it's your fault. Listen up! I have now proclaimed all over the neighbourhood that there is a pest that has arrived, so everyone must be ready. God knows what those niggers will send next. This is just the beginning of the end. Come quickly and I'll show you the nits that have now infested my house. And these are not normal nits, I can tell you that now! I have seen nits before, during the war, and they surely did not look like these. These are too big to be Norwegian nits. These are long and grey, these nits are from the continent far away, these are from the niggers." She pulled out a clean jam jar, where she had collected about five nits from the twins' heads. "I will report this to the authorities and warn them of the epidemic that is about to hit this nation."

I was just too tired to respond to her ridiculous behaviour and too drained to argue with her. The only thing I was able to do was laugh, watching the twins jump around very excited whilst laughing their heads off. That they had managed to get this reaction from Nan, they thought was very funny. Nan spent the rest of the day dealing with the nits she thought were crawling from floor to ceiling. I had to help her bang the rugs and all her cushions and get the entire house sorted out. I was totally drained after the previous night's event and I could not wait to get to bed to try to sleep it all off and forget about everything, and that was exactly what I did.

A few days later I went to town and met up with the people

I used to hang with. We all just wandered the streets for hours before we went up to the "open" house again to look for more alcohol and to see what went on. Apparently Steven had been taken to hospital where he had been for three days. He had passed out and was on his way to succeeding in his suicide attempt by destroying his liver. I must admit I was very happy to hear the news and I hoped he would not make it; I thought, "I hope the bastard is suffering."

I don't know why and how I did it, but I stayed at that house for almost a month just drinking and not caring about anything anymore. I had changed; I don't know what had happened to me on the inside to become what I became. It was totally wild in that house and the smell became absolutely horrible; people didn't even bother to go to the toilet. They did what they needed to in the hallway or the living room and I am not talking just urination. I think the house got totally destroyed. People were having sex in all the bedrooms. They were emptying all the freezers of food. In the huge basement, there were bottles stacked to the ceiling. When Kenny, the 19 year old son of the owner of the house, came back, he spent 40 000 kr (£4000) on alcohol. I was there drinking for a whole month, ending up as Kenny's girlfriend. I had no ownership over my body and when Kenny wanted sex I didn't care. I felt I no longer had the right to say no.

Finally Mum and Dad arrived and I went home, to a totally different life from what I had experienced for the last month. No more daily alcohol and once again the weekly routine of total monotony embraced my life. By then I had built up a front that completely hid my emotions; though I was a mess on the inside, I appeared to be a person who didn't care about anything.

Chapter 25

LEAVING HOME

The day arrived that I had been waiting for as long as I could remember, my last day at school, June 1982. I had passed my exam and my grades were okay, but sadly not good enough. I had 16 subjects, and scored B on 14 of them and C on 2. During the last year in school I had decided to work very hard to get good grades. I wanted to become a hairdresser and I knew I needed to do well for that. I had sent in application forms to schools all over the country, but sadly I didn't get accepted—I was too young, and I didn't have high enough scores in maths and physics.

My very first job was as an "au pair" about 40 miles from home. I just took the first job I was offered to get away. It was a disaster. I was only 16 years old and was responsible for three small three kids. When the parents went to work it was going to be my job to get two of the kids off to school and look after a six month old baby all day.

In those days many people didn't use paper nappies but all fabric. The first horrendous sight that met me in their house was in their basement. There in the utility was a big barrel of water filled to the top with fabric nappies—with all the contents of the nappies still in them! The man of the house said to me, "You will be cleaning those." Two of my sisters had had babies by now and I had helped them change the babies when they were home visiting. But we never left nappies to soak with their contents still in them.

I had long been aware of what was hygienic. I had to clean the whole house, and make sure dinner for the family was ready when they came home from work. I was hopeless about waking up in the morning because of my sleeping problems, and it was a nightmare to get up to all the responsibility that was put on me. There was no way I could run an entire home with all its chores, especially with all the emotional struggles I was going through. I suffered with so many thoughts and memories that haunted me from the past.

In the job as an au pair I felt like a slave, earning only 1000 krone (£100) a month. It was just too big a task for me at the time. I knew I had to find another job after being there just a few days.

Prior to taking the au pair job, I had planned to go on holiday with Mum to visit Angela down south. The family I worked for knew I was going to be away after just two weeks starting with them so they had prepared for that. I had always wanted to get work at the factory where Angela was working; the job as a housekeeper/au pair was just something I took in case I didn't get a job at the factory. I wanted to be sure to get away from home so I had jumped into the first thing available. I didn't tell the family I worked for about my intentions of going away, but I didn't care. I needed to sort my life out and it was definitely not going to be sorted out as a slave.

Mum and I drove the 350 mile trip down to the south of Norway on a Friday afternoon. First thing Monday morning I went to the factory and asked to see the man in charge of employment. His name was Adam. He stuttered, and I had great problems keeping a serious face when I talked to him. He stuttered away saying there was no work for me at this time, I was too young; I needed to be 18 to work at their machines. I was totally gutted, but determined not to give up. There was no way I wanted to go back to be a housekeeper looking after three kids. The following morning I went again, and I walked without appointment to his door. He smiled when he saw me. "Hi, you again?" he said. "Yes, me again," I said. "Can you please check if there is ANY work for me anywhere in this factory? I'll do anything, I don't care what. Just give me anything, please." Sadly, I got the same answer as I did the day before.

When horror pictures popped up in my mind of dirty nappies and floating turds in the big barrel of water, I got even more determined to nag Adam till I got a job; the only way he was going to get rid of me was by giving me work! So I went to see Adam again, and did the same thing on the Wednesday, receiving the same answer. I repeated my visit to him on the Thursday, without getting any nearer success. Finally Friday arrived; Mum was going home later in the evening and this was my last chance. So I did as I had done the last four days, I went to see Adam in his office. He looked up from behind his desk and his eyes actually lit up when he saw me. "Well, this isn't a surprise—you again!"

I pleaded with him, "This afternoon Mum is leaving and this is my last chance to move away from home. You have to find work for me. There has to be something I can do in this factory. What about sweeping the floors or stacking things? There has got to be something you can find for me to do. I know I am small and thin, but don't get fooled by that. Wait till you see how fast

I am and what a good worker I am! All my siblings are small and thin and they all have worked for this factory chain and have a good reputation of working twice as fast as anyone else. I will prove to you I can do the same."

By now Adam was laughing and threw himself back in his chair, "Okay, I'll see if I can find something for you to do. You don't give up, do you? Soon you will nag a big whole in my head, so I have to give you work, but I will only give you a two month contract. If you don't show me you work as you say you do, you will be without work in two months. You can start next Monday."

I jumped off my chair and shouted, "Yippee! I'll show you, I will work harder than anyone you have ever seen before." If it hadn't been for my ears, I am sure the smile on my face would have reached all around my head.

I had one week to prepare my move, before my work started. I went with Mum back home and packed my stuff. I didn't have any cutlery or saucepans or cups or plates. For my birthday a girlfriend had given me four lovely soup bowls and Granny had given me a coffee percolator, as I was a big coffee fan. I knew I needed kitchen things living by myself. As I was packing I went downstairs to ask her Mum if I could have one of her small saucepans so I could cook dinner for myself, saying that was the only meal I really was addicted to. I also asked her for some breakfast plates and the very few essentials that you would need when you start off in life. Mum refused to give me anything; she said she needed everything herself, full stop. I was not surprised. There was no point in trying to convince her that I needed something I could make food in and something to eat my food from. As always I knew I had to provide for myself.

I knew I was not going to get wages from the factory for

a while and the money I had saved up would go fast. I needed money to rent a room and I didn't know how much that was going to cost and I also needed money to put an advert in the newspaper to rent a room. Even though I had become a good thief I could not steal everything. I had never stolen kitchen appliances before so I had to try to find another solution for now.

I thought to myself, I have to contact Granny, she will help me out. Granny had moved out long ago, but she still had her stuff stored in a room at the farm. I rang Granny and said I was leaving home, going all the way down south. A couple of days later Granny came with Auntie Sara for a visit and to say goodbye to me. I asked if she could help me with something to get started. Granny was always generous. She gave me three breakfast plates, one small saucepan (I still use it today), a knife, a fork, a teaspoon, and a mug. My worries were now taken care of how I was going to consume my food. I packed all my belongings carefully in a big cardboard box measuring about 3x3 feet.

The following day Dad drove me to the lorry depot about 55 miles away and dropped me off so I could get a lift for free. These lorries worked for the factory chain that just had employed me, and they went down south to the "sister factory" where I was going to be working. Mum and Dad didn't give me any money or asked me if I needed anything before I left on the 350 miles long journey from home.

I was glad, though, when Dad agreed to take me 55 miles to the truck depot. This was the first thing he had done for me up to that point when I left home. I didn't know who was going to drive the lorry, but luckily it turned out that Dad knew him. Before Dad returned home he helped the lorry driver load my cardboard box. I jumped up into the passenger seat, over the moon with happiness that I was finally leaving home. Dad wished me a good trip before he got into his car and drove off. It still took quite a while before the lorry driver was finished with his paperwork and we could start the long journey, and there were lots of stops before I arrived at my destination eight hours later. But the day had finally arrived that I had been longing for so badly. I was free at last, and I loved the thought of never having to live at the farm again.

I lived at Angela's flat for two weeks before I got lucky enough to find a place to rent. I found a place that cost 1000 krone (£100) a month to rent, one third of my wages. I didn't get paid before I had worked there for two weeks, and I then had only 750 krone (£75). I was paid minimal wages, only 1.50£ an hour. But I soon got higher wages. Within just a few weeks I kept my word to Adam, and he had found a machine I was allowed to use, even though I was only 16. I proved to be a hard worker; in fact, I passed the production amount of others who had worked there for years. My job was upholstering seats of dining room chairs. I was as fast as a lunatic, and after the two months I got to keep my job. I rode my bike two miles to work, where I started at 7 am and finished at 3.30 pm. When I came home, I was alone all evening and did the same the next morning, day in and day out. But at least I was finally away from home; I had my own place and was earning money to save up to go to college to become a hairdresser.

Even though I had for so long looked forward to moving away from home, I still faced some challenges. Especially at the weekends, I was so bored that I used to party a lot. I didn't know many people down south except one girl I had met up north, but she was a bit empty headed and I wasn't fussed on spending too much time with her. I eventually got to know some people in the factory that invited me to party with them. I joined them for a few parties, but I wasn't keen; I felt I didn't fit into their crowd. I discovered at some parties people were smoking hashish. In the west of Norway I knew of no one that did that. I thought that hashish users were the total losers of society; in my perspective, they were drug addicts and junkies. I wanted to have nothing to do with people that were doing drugs. Most of the time I just worked and slept.

Autumn went into winter and Christmas was fast approaching. Christmas of 1982 was the last time I spent with Mum and Dad, even though I was just 16. I looked forward to having a good break from the factory and resting up. Angela and I went back home to celebrate the festive season at the farm, but about 40 miles before we arrived home my stomach started churning and I felt sick. It was actually hurting, as if a knife was hitting my guts, just from the thought of going back to the house. The palms of my hands got wet and I was shaking inside and I became incredibly anxious. I felt this way every time I went back home, until I reached the age of 27 and something happened that would change my life for ever.

I was very happy to see Granny again, though; I had missed her tremendously. As always, though, my parents were drinking and tension between Mum and Granny was building up. Granny only stayed the night of Christmas Eve before she left for Sara's. I didn't like Christmas at all. I had almost forgotten the horrible atmosphere haunting that house. There was always a sense that something evil was right behind, no matter where you turned. It took me about two days before I got used to the horrible feeling that haunted me in the house and I didn't go to bed scared stiff. I didn't stay long, maybe for about six days because I had planned to go to the big city together with a girl I had gotten to know from the north and celebrate New Year's Eve. Even though I was quite lonely living alone and knowing very few people down south, I could not wait to leave the farm and get away.

Chapter 26

THE WRONG CROWD

Finally New Year's Eve arrived. I was ready for a party. I had gotten to know Sandy, from the years on holidays up north, and I had caught up with her where she lived down south. Sandy said it was going to be very exciting to spend the evening in the city because of all the parties that would be held there. She said there would be no problem for us to find a crowd, and where there was a crowd there would soon be a party. After loads of dolling up we were ready for some action and took the train to the city to see if we could find some wild party to join.

It was a freezing cold night, below 24c. We walked up and down the streets covered with snow, hoping we would find a crowd we could join. The cold went right through all my clothes, even though I was wearing long johns under my jeans and several layers on the top too. I was shivering right through my whole body, and I hated every minute of it. After walking up and down the totally dead main street for over an hour, I had had enough.

It turned out that we were too young to be allowed into any of the discos in the city. The age requirement was 18 and most of the discos were shut anyway. Soon I realised what a stupid idea it was to go to the capital to find a place to have fun, especially on such a cold night; all the people obviously had their own private home parties. I became irritated and said to Sandy, "You used to live in the city—why on earth did you invite me to come down here when there is nobody here?" I told Sandy I had had enough.

Luckily we managed to catch the last train home. It was only about 10 pm and it looked like our New Year's Eve was doomed. But our luck was about to turn around. On the train we met some other girls we never had seen before. We started to joke around with them, and we really hit it off. The girls laughed when they heard where we had been. They said it was a dead city for people our age. The girls were on their way to a private party and said we could come with them if we wanted to. They weren't sure if those who held the party would let two new girls in, but they said it was up to us if we wanted to take the risk. The party was about five stops from our stop and I said to Sandy, "What the heck. Let's chance it. Make sure to look very innocent and keep your mouth shut, and then they'll let us in." I knew if Sandy opened her mouth she would blow it. We jumped off the train at their stop, excited at finding two new friends and also finally getting to go to a New Year's Eve party we had been looking for all night.

As we arrived at the party and the girls rang the doorbell, a young woman about 22 years old opened the door and the girls asked as kindly as they could, if all four of us could join them. The young woman looked us up from top to toe before she nodded and said, "Okay, I'll let you in, but make sure you all behave." I saw she was very careful of who was allowed to come in and didn't just open the door to everyone. Yet even with her effort, it didn't take long before the party got out of hand; people just started to stream in from everywhere.

It soon became a very wild party. There were people everywhere, music blasting, the sound of glass smashing onto the tiled floor. Obviously the parents were not home, and the house had been entrusted to the young adults in the house. The woman who opened the door really tried to control what was happening, but she didn't stand a chance with all her younger brother Jim's friends joining the party. I knew there were no more trains running until the next morning and I just hoped to not get kicked out into the freezing cold night. I didn't break any glasses or destroy anything like I heard all around me. I kept wondering if there would be any glasses left in the morning that were not broken and I thought how gutted the owners of the house would be when they found their house in such a state. But I continued to dance, and I had great fun.

I also entertained people by doing fortune telling, I had taken great interest in this subject at a young age, and I had learned to read the palm of the hand and also ordinary cards. It was always a great attraction at the parties when people found out I could read about their future and tell them what I saw when I read their hands, and very often I was spot on about things they had been through.

Between the fortune telling and dancing I got quite drunk, but I was still able to spot Jim. It was not difficult because he was a very tall guy, and it was fun to see him try to dance. He was jumping around on crutches and it was a hilarious sight seeing him try to manoeuvre his way around on the dance floor. Apparently seven months earlier Jim had been hospitalised for several months after a very serious motorbike accident which he miraculously survived. Jim and I hit it off very well. I liked him immediately even though I felt he was far too tall for me.

I don't remember what we talked about, but we ended up

kissing, and though it was just a party flirt, I still ended up in bed with him. I didn't care that Jim was a stranger. I had come to terms with the "fact" that I didn't own my body, so I had sex with him, as I usually did when a boy wanted it. In a strange way I felt obligated to do so, and I also thought it was expected of me. I got something in return. I longed for attention, and I wanted to be attractive, and I craved being wanted by someone. Most of all, I wanted to be loved. Sadly, I didn't understand that sex like this had nothing to do with love.

The next morning, very early, I was awakened by Sandy shouting, "Laila, Laila, where are you? I am going home. Come on, we need to go." I got very embarrassed and when Jim asked me what was going on I said, "She is just a nut case and I don't want to have anything to do with her." Sandy kept shouting, but I didn't bother to answer. I had a massive hangover from the previous night and the last thing I wanted was to see her. By now I was tired of her and hoped she would just leave. I had used her as an emergency friend in the first place. I went with Sandy because I didn't know anyone else. Finally Sandy stopped shouting, and I heard the front door slam and I knew she was off. A few hours later I sobered up and Jim asked me where I lived so he could take me home. Even though he was on crutches he still was able to drive the car, not legally of course, as he used his crutch to pull the gas pedal. He dropped me off outside where I lived, and I didn't see or hear from him again for three months.

I had turned 17 in February and about six weeks after, right before Easter, I heard a knock on my door, and there stood Jim, as tall as a skyscraper. I had not thought much about Jim at all, but when he asked if he could come in, I laughed and said, "Welcome, long time no see." I made some coffee and we chatted for a few hours before he asked me if I wanted to go for a drive. When I saw his car again I went totally up the sky because I loved American cars and he had a Dodge Dart! I felt very proud and that I had laid the golden egg, riding in an American car with a good looking boy.

We started to hang out together more and more. I fell in love with him very soon, and every day I went to work I had something to look forward to. I could not wait to see him when he popped in to visit me. Soon he stayed over and sometimes he was there when I came from work too. He had loads of friends and I didn't realise at first the kind they were. I was just relieved that I didn't have to be alone anymore. I finally was able to be a part of a group and have friends to go around with and have fun.

I went to several parties with him where I soon discovered all his friends were smoking dope. I knew very little about dope, but the little I knew made me hate it. Listening to music one night at a party, a cigarette was passed my way. I said, "No thanks, I don't smoke," and the cigarette was passed to the next one. I asked Jim, "Why are they sharing that cigarette? Why don't they roll their own?" Jim explained that it was not an ordinary cigarette, it was "gangi". I didn't know what gangi was. I only knew the word hashish and didn't know any other nicknames for it. Jim laughed at my naiveté, and told me it was hashish. The great hatred I had towards drugs ignited in me again and I jumped up in anger and said, "Take me out of here. There is no way I am spending time with losers." I asked if he was smoking that stuff too, because then he could forget about us. Jim reassured me that he had quit dope months ago.

As much as I wanted to leave immediately, there was no way for me to leave the party. Jim could not drive, and he had been drinking as well, so I was stuck. I was very angry, knowing the people around me were smoking dope, so I went into one of the bedrooms away from the group. As usual I found it very difficult to fall asleep, even though I had been drinking spirit, but eventually I slept and woke very early in the morning and woke up Jim and asked him to take me home.

A few weeks later Jim and I were sitting in his car talking whilst he was dropping me off at home. His face became very serious and he said he had something to confess to me. I instantly went on red alert, expecting to hear that he had found another girl. Jim looked down at his lap, and then his face went bright red when he confessed, "I am so sorry, Laila, but at that party we went to a few weeks ago, I smoked dope." Inside I was relieved that he had not gone with another girl, but anger rose up inside me with the thought of the dope he had been doing. With blazing eyes I turned on him and shouted, "You can do what the hell you want with your life, but I will not be in it. I am never going to be with a person who is a loser and takes drugs." I raced out of the car shouting, "Get the hell out of my life, goodbye." I slammed the door behind me and ran into my room. I threw myself on my bed and cried, thinking this is typical of me, finally falling in love and he turns out to be a "drug addict".

The next day Jim came and knocked at my door again. I was very tired because I had not had a very good sleep and I had worked very hard all day at the factory. I wasn't exactly glad to see him, but I let him in because I had missed him even though I was still angry and hurt. I don't know why I had such hatred towards drugs, but I know now that that hatred protected me. If I had not had such hatred, with my broken background and my extreme non stop personality, I would have gone the whole way, not just doing hashish, and probably would have ended up dead like many of Jim's friends eventually did.

Jim began to spend the nights quite regularly at my place. One day I had gone to work at 6.30 in the morning and I could not wait till I got home to see Jim. I rode my bike up all the long hills to my home. When I approached my entrance I heard laughing and loud music. I let myself in only to find Jim with four of his dope smoking friends in my room. The whole room was grey with hashish-smelling smoke, and beer bottles filled the small coffee table. Jim's friends were very friendly. As I walked into my room, they said, "Oh, look who is here, the lady of the house. Have a beer—you must be thirsty."

My anger fuse lit instantly. I exploded like a volcano spewing out its pyroclastic hot cloud. Jim had had let these people in while I was working my arse off at the factory. He had not given one thought of the repercussions to me personally. He knew very well my view of these dope people. I had trusted Jim to stay there while I was not home. I knew I was risking getting chucked out by my landlord. I was living in a private house where they had made a room with an en suite in their basement. Even though I had my own entrance to my room, it was easy for my landlord to hear that there was a party downstairs.

I shouted to all of them to "get the hell out of my room now, or I will call the police. This is not a hashish dive, this is my home, which I pay for, with my money that I have been working my arse off for, you f***ing lazy scumbag losers. Get the f*** out of my sight right now." I screamed so loud that they all shot up and out the door. I shouted to Jim also to get the "f*** out of my house and out of my life." He tried to explain that he was only drinking beer, but I didn't care. He had brought a gang of losers into my home and I was risking getting chucked out and that was enough for me. I was so upset when they all left my hands were shaking. I didn't know how I could have been so stupid to get involved with a guy that had such friends. I remembered Granddad used to say, "Show me your friends and I will tell you who you are." That was a fact for me, and I was so gutted because I had fallen in love with Jim.

A couple of days later Jim knocked at the door and pleaded to come in. When I opened the door, his face was bright red and he was crying. He said he didn't want to lose me and that he loved me. He said he was going to finish with the gang; he saw that they were losers and he wanted to sort his own life out. He said he had seen how hard I was working and it had made him wake up, to see that I was not even living home with my parents, like him, getting food ready on the table every day. He said I had opened his eyes, and that he understood there was another life to live other than what he was living and he wanted to grow up. He said my life had shown him such a contrast to what he had been used to. He was so sorry to have put me at risk of losing my home. I saw he genuinely meant what he was saying, and I forgave him immediately, relieved that he was back because I was so in love with him.

A few lovely quiet weeks followed where we only spent time with his best friend and his girlfriend, drinking only beer at weekends when we wanted to have fun. I told Jim that if he wanted to make something out of his life, I could help him. I told him how I had saved up all my money to move away far from home and how I got the job at the factory. I stressed to him the importance of persevering and doing what it takes to get where you want. I said there are ways you can become something, and one way to start is to get a job soon. Jim had come off his crutches and was just walking with a limp. "Just apply for any work you can get," I told him, "and work your way up."

It didn't take Jim long to find work. He got a job at a food store, worked very hard, and eventually became the manager of the shop. The only thing I really did for Jim was give him the encouragement he needed to get his life right. I helped him see that it was possible to change his own life. The motorbike accident didn't need to rule the rest of his life. I believe I set a personal example for Jim because I had been able to do it with my back ground.

Chapter 27

PREGNANT

I remember the first time I was introduced to Jim's parents. It was in the summer of 1983. I had never really dated anyone properly before, so this was the first time I was going to meet some boy's parents. It was such a lovely, hot, sunny day that we just walked around the back of his house into a very large garden. I was nervous and I didn't know what to say or do in meeting Jim's parents. It turned out there was no need for me to be scared. The moment Jim's mum saw us she lit up and said, "We finally get to meet the girl our son has talked so much about! We have been so curious about this mysterious girl that has turned our son's life around to the good."

With that she came towards me and gave me a big, warm hug. As she put her arms tight around me, I froze and stood stiff as a stick, terrified of such affection. I don't think she noticed that I didn't hug her back; I was relieved when she finally let me go and offered me some mango ice tea. I had never heard about ice tea before, and it sounded lovely, like it had ice cream in it, but when I sipped the cup I was disappointed to discover it was only cold tea. I didn't like it at all, but tried to hide the expression on my face.

Jim's parents were a Godsend. Over the next few years I was able to learn from Jim's parents how to receive and give physical affection. Every time I met them they would give me a warm, tight hug, and in the end I got so used to it I even started to fold my arms around them and hug them back. Through his parents I also learned some manners!

Most importantly, they were a wonderful example to me, showing harmony in their family which I had never seen before. This was the first time I had experienced being around a normal family. At only 17 years old, I think I adopted them in my mind as my "parents," or mentors, if you like. I still have a very close relationship with them today, even after all these years.

By the autumn of 1983 I had decided to apply for college again, and I went to Adam at the factory to ask if I could have one year's leave so I could attempt to go to college. I told him I wasn't sure I would be able to become a hairdresser, because of my constant back pain. But I wanted to at least have a go, so I knew I had tried. I was allowed to have one year of unpaid leave, and if it didn't work out for me as a hairdresser, I could come back to work at the factory.

By the autumn Jim sold his Dodge Dart to get money for the deposit and we bought our first one bedroom flat. It had an open plan, with a living room, kitchen, bathroom, and a large airing cupboard. Finally we started living together. I applied for a student loan, and I used the money to buy some furniture for our flat. Jim was starting to earn good money, but we still had to watch every penny, as we had taken on a mortgage. I was accepted at college and started the course of hairdressing which had been my dream since I was a little girl, combing Granny's hair. I could still hear her encouraging words, "You will make a wonderful hairdresser, Laila."

It was a tough year. There was no easy way to get to college. First, I had to walk one mile to get to the bus stop, and then there was a one and half hour journey each way on busses and trains, and then I would walk ½ mile to the college from the bus stop. I was constantly tired and suffered from terrible insomnia. In 1983 college was totally different than it is today. I had five lessons a day, five days a week for a whole year, before I was even allowed to start as a hairdressing trainee. Still I loved it and finally I was doing something I had dreamt of for so many years. My life had never been easy anyway; I knew that if I wanted something, the only way to get it was to work hard for it.

New Year's Eve approached. Walking the streets one day, Jim and I passed a jeweller and I said, "Look at that lovely jewellery." Jim said, "Would you like one of those rings?" When I said yes, there and then we decided to get engaged on New Year's Eve 1983. It would mark the one year anniversary of when we first met.

A couple of months after we got engaged, I found out I was pregnant. I was only 18 years old. The doctors had told me to stop using the pill I had been on for just a few months, because I had suffered from so much pain in my womb since I started on them. I was still in college training for hairdressing, and as the months went by, I was totally exhausted, with the long journey and all. The constant smell of perm liquids and other sickly hairsprays added to my misery. I was not in good shape for the first few months of my pregnancy. My back was killing me, and I had mood swings worse than I can describe.

There was another change that happened when I got pregnant. My days as a thief were over. There was no way I dared to steal one more thing at the shops. I was petrified just by the thought of stealing something. I had stolen a lot of stuff for our flat when Jim and I moved in together, everything from curtains to beddings, towel rails, and all sorts of other essentials. But being pregnant made me freeze just thinking about stealing something. My heart would race even at the sight of a police car. I guess I finally realized the consequences if I got caught, and now I had a baby to be thinking of.

I completed only the first year at college. If I wanted to complete my education and become a hairdresser, in my second year I would have to spend three days as a trainee and two days at college. I was four months pregnant when I started as a trainee. I only worked there for a few weeks because I was exhausted from standing on my feet all day, with constant back pain. The worst part of being a trainee was that they only allowed me to cut the hair of toddlers. That was the most difficult kind of customer I ever had. It took 100 times more energy to make them sit still, and with them turning their heads all the time, I had to be careful not to miss and cut their flesh. I handed in my resignation after just two weeks knowing there was no way for me to continue, with what was wrong with my back. With that I ended my education. But I finally was able to get rest and well needed sleep. I wanted to put all my energy into motherhood.

One night Jim and I were relaxing watching telly. As I was stroking my growing belly, I said to Jim, "I think we should get married, with us expecting a baby and all. I don't feel we would be real and proper parents just living together. It's not like we are going to split up, is it? Now that we have our own flat and also a baby on the way, I think we might as well get married, don't you think so, too?" Jim said, That's okay with me," so nine weeks later and with about 30 guests present, Jim and I stood bride and groom, both of us naively and childishly trying to do life together the best we could. I had just turned 18 and Jim was only 20, and neither of us had the slightest clue about the rocky ride our marriage was going to be from the start.

I was finally old enough to start taking driving lessons. But I had to walk one mile to the bus stop and ride 20 minutes on the bus to get to do my lesson, then catch the bus and walk home from the bus stop. I was very distracted and spaced out when I was pregnant. I often walked the mile down a steep hill to take the bus, only to find out I had forgotten to take money for the bus fare. Then I had to hitchhike to get to my driving lesson, something I didn't like to do since I moved away from the west.

Thankfully Jim earned enough money to provide for us, but I hardly saw him. He worked all the time, and I was alone in the apartment all day. It was so hot in the summer and I didn't even dare to go out on my balcony because wasps were swirling everywhere, and I was terrified of them. There were no greens I was able to go out to either. The people downstairs had a lawn, but that was their private one. My back was so bad I could not walk long distances and I ended up on my own inside the flat, seeing no one day in and out while Jim was working.

Being alone and feeling very lonely gave me loads of time to meditate on my broken childhood. I felt so lost. Now and again I had visitors from the Jehovah's Witnesses and I gladly let them in to have someone to talk to. The JW came regularly for a number of months and were very nice people. I even bought a Bible from them, but trying to read it made no sense to me. The more they came to visit me, the more I became afraid of dying, thinking I was doomed. When I asked them questions they were not able to give me the answers that I so much longed for. I became totally depressed as I meditated over the years I had lost as a kid, and I dug myself into a deep, dark hole of self pity.

There were some highlights in my first pregnancy, though. I finally passed my driving test and Jim bought me a cheap Lada. Then I was able to get out of the house on some occasions, that is, if the Lada decided to start!

The 12th of November I went into labour at 2 am and four hours later my oldest son Frank was born. As soon as I had delivered him and he was put on my stomach, an overwhelming sense of love came over me as I gazed down on the little pitch black hair of my newborn. Looking at this innocent little child, totally helpless and depending on me as a mum to look after him, threw me into a mixture of fear and grief—how on earth was I going to be a good mum for my little newborn son?

Frank grew quickly and I went for regular checks at the clinic to have him weighed. The health visitor/nurse was very helpful and I took in every word she said to learn how to look after Frank. Soon the nurse said Frank needed to take his jabs and I took him regularly to the clinic to have them done. One day as I was talking to the nurse, I told her that I have never taken any jabs when I grew up. She thought I was kidding at first, but I said all the kids in school had it done, but I was always put aside because I never had a health card when I was little. Apparently Mum never took me to these clinics to get weighed or for my jabs for any of the childhood sicknesses like rubella and polio. The nurse said I definitely needed to take them, too, so at the age of 18 1/2 I started to get all of my vaccinations done. In one way I felt I was growing up together with my son, when we took our jabs together.

At this time I started more and more to relive my childhood.

As I watched my son take his first brave steps, I wondered how it was for me when I was little. Did my brother treat me bad even then? Was I unwanted by Dad when I was learning to walk? I couldn't remember.

When Frank was only eight months old I became pregnant again. Jim had a great position as a manager at the shop but he wanted to do further education so he could start his own business. I pleaded with Jim to postpone this till our second baby was born, as I felt I needed him more now that I was pregnant again. The last thing I wanted was to be alone all the time with Frank. I wanted us to be a family and for Frank to be able to see his dad. Jim left for work before Frank was up, and he wasn't home before 10 pm in the evenings. Jim worked very hard, and I know he was under a lot of pressure with such long days, but I felt we were slipping more and more apart. I felt like a married, single mother.

But Jim was determined. He said it wouldn't be much different—he would study on the side and work full time and I would see him more. Of course that was not the case. We saw less and less of each other and our marriage was deteriorating rapidly. Expecting another baby also forced us to find another, bigger flat. The prices had gone up the year we lived in our brand new flat, so we sold our flat at a great profit. We bought a 96 square meter apartment on the first floor with three bedrooms, in a less attractive area where it was still cheap. But I loved the new flat. It had lovely large green gardens where I could take Frank out to play, and I became friends with a woman on the ground floor called Kate. We were outside all day watching our kids play.

During my second pregnancy I wasn't as depressed as in my first one, and having the new friend downstairs made my days less lonely. Also I had a kind of friend in Frank; he became my living doll. I wanted to do everything right, and I followed the textbook to the letter. I tried to compensate for what I had lost as a child to make my son's childhood right. I gave Frank everything I had longed for myself as a kid. When I put Frank down for a nap I used to sit on the floor and hold his hand while stroking his head gently till he fell asleep. I sang lullabies to him and told him fairytales even though he could not speak. I never spoke baby language to him; I spoke to him as an adult and wanted him to learn the correct way of speaking from the beginning. I breastfed him till he was eight months old, then I had to stop because he found it funny to bite my nipple during his feed, laughing his head off when I screamed out in pain. I cooked homemade baby food for him and even started to brush his gums before he had teeth so he could get used to the toothbrush. I always played on the floor with Frank and I almost became a child myself, trying to take back what I had lost, the childhood that was stolen.

I know I was very demanding to Jim, the little time he spent at home. And I had started to distrust him. He was away so much, and he seemed less and less interested in family life and me. When he was home he only wanted to watch TV or read the newspaper. It didn't make things better when he sometimes received phone calls during which he blushed red like a tomato. The way he spoke on the phone didn't sound like he was speaking to a man, and I became more and more jealous that he might be seeing other women at work.

With our marriage deteriorating already in our honeymoon days, I just threw myself into the role as a mum, but with great difficulties. There were times when Frank would fall and hurt himself, and I would run up as fast as I could to cuddle him and comfort him till he stopped crying. In those moments I went back to my own childhood. I revisited times when I needed comforting but never was given any. As I hugged and cuddled Frank, I was crying inside myself, realizing my childhood had been taken from me, and I didn't know how to take it back. I spent more and more time meditating on the past and destroyed my present in doing so.

Chapter 28

IT'S YOUR FAULT

On the 7th of April 1986 my daughter Miriam was born. I had just passed my 20th birthday and now I was a mother of two. This time I had a 12 hour labour, and the umbilical cord was wrapped around Miriam's neck twice so she was quite blue when she was born. But after a few hours in the incubator she was fine. Frank was the proudest big brother ever. He had a little sister and now he was one year and five months old and he spoke almost fluently.

When Miriam was only two months old I decided to visit Mum and Dad again so that they could see their new grand child. I said to Mum that I would not come to the farm if they were drinking. Mum said they had no drinks there now and they had not been drinking for a while anyway, and she promised not to drink. My oldest sister gave me advice about what she did if Mum and Dad were drinking when she visited—she said she just left. I thought to myself that threatening to leave might stop them from starting to drink this time. I told Mum if they started to drink I would leave immediately because I didn't want my kids exposed to their drinking and fighting.

This time Mum came and picked me up at the airport on Thursday the 5th of June 1986. I was very anxious because the airport was located in the city where she could get hold of her gin. On the two hour drive back to the farm, Mum immediately started to smoke in the car. I begged her not to because of my little baby and Frank, but she said that it was no problem because she could open the window. She made a ½ inch gap on her front window in the car, and the smoke soon filled the car on the long journey home. I thought to myself, nothing has changed here; no thought that this might be unhealthy for little children. Just as they smoked when I was a child, they continued to smoke without a care in the presence of my children.

We arrived at the farm and I sorted my kids out and changed their nappies and gave Frank his food. Mum was sitting in the living room crocheting two white bases for the bridesmaids' flowers for one of my sister's wedding the following month. I walked in the door holding Miriam in my arms about to nurse her. As I sat down I gazed towards Mum, and I saw that her face that was once beautiful, was now bloated, and she was very pale with dark circles underneath her eyes. Her face was drawn and wrinkled. She had always been skinny, but now her body was skin and bones. In a micro second I looked at her and thought that she was dying. "Mum will be dead soon," I thought to myself. I tried to chase away the thoughts by just commenting on the thing she was crocheting.

Later that evening, I had just gotten Frank off to sleep, and was trying to get Miriam settled. My heart sunk when I heard Mum and Dad starting to shout in the living room next door. The familiar sound of angry, drunk voices was breaking through the thick timber walls. I looked at my two little ones feeling trapped.

I clung on to Miriam and held her as tight as I could, wanting to protect her from the shouting. I was shaking all over. Though I knew the anger wasn't aimed at me, this was an echo from my childhood, and I was instantly transported back in time and became a frightened little girl again.

When I felt the coast was clear, I ran into the other living room where the phone was and rang my auntie Sara to see if she could please pick me up the following morning and if I could stay with her for the rest of my visit. I explained the situation and she said she would be there first thing in the morning. It was too late to leave that night because Frank and Miriam had already fallen asleep.

Luckily Mum and Dad calmed down eventually, and there was no big fight between them that night. It turned out that they had shouted about some other people that had ticked them off, and it was an ongoing thing that had been frustrating them. However, just hearing any form of shouting from them still brought back the fear I had lived under as a child. I was so disappointed with Mum; she had promised me that they would not drink.

The following day Aunt Sara came to pick me up as I had asked her to do the night before. As I was getting my babies ready and putting the pram in the car, Mum and Dad walked down from the barn, getting a few sheep out into the mountains for the summer. I took out my camera and snapped a few pictures of her as she was walking with the sheep towards the house. Thoughts were racing through my mind telling me that these pictures would be the last pictures of Mum. I had such a strong sense she would be dead soon. I felt horror creep down my back as those thoughts went through my mind, and once again I tried to chase them away.

As I took the pictures of her, I saw that Mum was emotional; she was holding back tears. The expression on her face that

morning haunted me for many years. When Mum saw Sara's car
and she knew I was going, she told me that I was childish and I
should stop making my point. "We don't have any more alcohol
now," she said. "We drank it all yesterday." I wanted to believe
her, and I really didn't want to leave, since I felt she was in danger
of dying. I wanted to stay, but she hadn't kept her promise to me,
and now I felt I had to leave because that is what I had told her I
would do. Being torn by all those thoughts, I still stubbornly told
Mum she broke her promise not to drink, and I would not break
the promise that I had given her which was to leave if they did.
I said to her, "You can give me a call when you decide to stop
drinking. I might come back."

As I put my kids into Sara's car, I turned my head around to get
one last glimpse of Mum. I had a really strong feeling that Mum
was going to die, and even though I wanted to stay, I went against
my instincts and drove off with Sara. The decision to leave the day
after I had arrived on the farm, Friday, the 6th of June, made me live
in regret and torment for the next seven years.

The following evening on the Saturday, I rang Ted's phone;
he and his girlfriend were living in the upstairs apartment on the
farm. His girlfriend answered the phone and I asked if Mum and
Dad were still drinking. Ted's girlfriend said they had gone on a
binge; Mum had come into their living room and asked if they
had any alcohol. Ted had a bottle of whisky and Mum filled a
tall glass with it, topped it up with a tiny drop of water, and then
gulped it down in one go. After three of those she wobbled back
out the door, hardly able to walk.

I was so afraid that Mum would die that I rang Sunday,
Monday, and Tuesday evenings to hear if Mum and Dad had
stopped drinking so that I could go back to the farm. On the

Wednesday evening, five days after I had left the farm, I received a phone call from Ted around 9 pm. He told me that Mum was dying. The first thought that went through my mind was that she had tried to commit suicide again. I didn't quite comprehend what was happening and I didn't even believe it was true – my fears had become a reality.

I am normally very fast and can get ready in the wink of an eye, but this time I could not sort out anything that I needed to return to the farm. Everything was in slow motion; it was as if I was in a dream. I asked my cousin Ken if he could look after Frank when he woke in the morning, I would only take the baby with me for now, and he agreed to help me out. I continued to pack Miriam's things, but what would normally take me 15 minutes, took me two hours before I was ready to leave for the farm. It was about a 40 minute drive to the farm, and when we had driven about halfway we met an ambulance. I said to Auntie Sara, "Mum is inside that ambulance and she is dead." Ted had only said on the phone that she was dying, but I just knew she was dead and was inside that ambulance. Sara didn't comment on what I said, she just continued to drive to the farm.

I can't remember what I did when I got there but I can remember what Dad said. He said that he had sobered up and had gone to work in the morning and saw that Mum was not well. He had asked her if she wanted a doctor but she told him that she just had a terrible hangover so he went to work. He said that when he came home at 4:30 pm, he found her still in bed and he saw that she had deteriorated badly. He struggled to keep her alive by breathing air into her mouth. He eventually had given up as her body shut down. She was throwing up and she was unable to keep what was in her bowels. He had eventually stormed out of the bedroom into Ted's living room saying that he couldn't handle it any longer.

I don't know who called the ambulance, if it was Ted who called it, then called me saying that Mum was about to die. Ted had run up and tried to rescue Mum without success. Mum was already dead by the time the ambulance arrived. The autopsy showed that Mum's suprarenal gland/adrenal gland had burst and it caused blood poisoning in her body, apparently a very fast and painful death.

It's impossible for me to describe what I was feeling during the days that followed. The pain was so bad that it was almost impossible to breathe. Jim came up from the south to join me, even though he had an exam he had to take. He was able to do it in a city up in the west due to the circumstances surrounding this death. Jim said we needed to take a walk up the hills to try to get away from the chaos at the house. That was when it suddenly dawned on me why Mum had been drinking. It was like a penny had dropped. I now knew why, but I didn't understand why I hadn't seen this before. Why didn't I accept it before she died? Now it was too late. If I had known this five days ago I would not have left the farm.

I suddenly realized that Mum spoke the truth when she said she had to drink to be able to relax. She was totally unable to relax without alcohol; it was so simple. Why hadn't I understood that while she was alive? Why hadn't I accepted that Mum had a problem? I had thought that if I punished her by leaving, then she might stop drinking. Now it was too late. I had left her and she was probably too depressed to stop drinking. I realised too late that I should have stayed and accepted that she was an alcoholic.

I felt so guilty for letting her down. She needed all the support

she could get from her children, but all I gave her was rejection.
I thought surely she would choose to be with her children and
grandchildren instead of the alcohol. By pushing her away I
thought I would bring her back. But why didn't I see that Mum
was sick? I had known inside for many years that Mum was an
alcoholic, but I had never really accepted that she was one. I had
always wanted her to stop drinking, but I didn't know that she was
not able to stop. I had believed she just had to make one decision,
to simply stop drinking, and she could get sober. I didn't realise
that alcoholism is a sickness, and that she needed help.

   I told Jim about my big mistake, how bad I had been and how
awful it must have been for Mum to have all her children leave
her because of her drinking problem. Jim didn't know what to
say to comfort me, and I knew that he only tried his best when he
said, "You should not be sad that your Mum is dead, the way you
have been treated. You should be glad she is dead; why are you
so sad?" A knife hit my guts and I wanted to throw up; he could
not be more wrong. My only mum was gone. I dissolved into
tears; there was no way for Jim to understand what was going on
inside of me and how I was torn apart by guilt.

   In those days, I was very superstitious. I remembered that
when I first arrived, I had looked at Mum and thought that she
would be dead soon. Now that she was dead, in a weird way, I
felt that I had sentenced her to death. I know it's crazy, but I felt
responsible for her death. All my chances of having a real mum
had now died with Mum. Even though she was an alcoholic,
she was still my mum and I had never given up hope of having a
relationship with her. I had lived in the hope that one day it would
all be restored. Even though I knew the hope was unrealistic, I
still had it buried in my heart.

The following day I had just put Frank to bed, and I passed Ted
in the hallway going downstairs. His eyes were filled with furious
fire when he shouted at me, "It's all your fault that Mum is dead!
You killed her! If you had not left to go to Sara's, Mum would still
be alive. Mum drank herself silly when you left, because you hurt
her so much by leaving. She was drowning her sorrows over you.
Do you hear me, Laila? It's YOUR FAULT she is dead!" Those
words haunted me day and night for many years, and I actually
believed them. In my mind I kept thinking, "It's my fault. I killed
Mum. She would be alive if I hadn't gone."

Chapter 29

BREAKING POINT

The funeral was awful; at the graveyard my siblings surrounded Dad holding onto him from all angles. I clung on to Auntie Wilma, Mum's sister, as she was standing on her own on the other side of the open grave. I felt very sorry for Wilma since she was Mum's only sister and they always had had a close relationship. I used to spend a lot of time with her every summer when I was teenager; she was the closest thing that I had to a mum.

I don't know how many days or even if it was weeks after Mum's funeral when we were all together in the living room chatting. Dad was drinking heavily at this point and he had already got very drunk. Suddenly he turned his head towards me and started to have a go at me. "On the saddest day of my life every single one of my children was around supporting their Dad except you, Laila. You stood by Wilma and not by me at the funeral; it just goes to show, Laila, that you are not my child. If you were my child, you would have stood next to me like the others."

I was unable to say a word. I just looked down at my lap. His words pierced my heart. I froze to ice. My heart pounded in my chest and I didn't know what to think or what to say, the pain was too intense. I was a young mother myself with two little ones, but I was in desperate need of a parent too. I had not only lost a mother I had never had a relationship with, but Dad still looked at me as the bastard of the family. I was still unwanted by my father. I felt my heart break into a thousand pieces.

The summer passed and I eventually went back down south to my own home. I had two little children to look after, but that didn't help me in my despair of missing Mum, a mum that I never had but so desperately wanted. Often I would dial the number of the farm and let it ring a few times, hoping Mum would answer the phone, and then I would hang up, pretending she was out. I didn't realize until much later that I simply hadn't accepted that she was dead.

Every night when I went to bed I lay on my side away from Jim, and I would quietly cry, hoping Jim did not hear me. I know it must have been difficult for Jim to know how to deal with my grief, but he never spoke about it and he never touched me or asked me if I was okay, or even said to me that it would be okay. He probably didn't want to upset me more. Jim just continued his own business and worked hard and probably did the best he could whilst still being away from home most of the time.

I started to have repeated nightmares about my Mum's death. This was about the time Michael Jackson released his famous "Thriller" video. When I saw the images of the deteriorating corpses in the music video I was petrified. All I was thinking of was death and now the video showed me what a dead person looks like. The video haunted me day and night. Not only was Mum dead, but now I had to cope with images in my mind of her rotting underground, like those images from "Thriller." At this time there was also a TV series called "V", about aliens, which also terrified me. I had always been fragile when it came to what I watched on TV or at the cinema and watching these shows had an immediate effect on my dreams. I had become so depressed that I was convinced that I had no right to live; I was the one that should have died, not Mum. I thought that I had to end my life to make it right. I needed a death sentence because I had killed Mum by leaving her when she probably needed me the most. If I died, that would be the punishment I deserved. I was trying to figure out a plan on how to end my life. Even though I had Frank and Miriam, it didn't fuel any desire in me to live.

I still had contact with my friend Kate who lived on the first floor. Kate saw the misery I was in, so she told me about a psychiatrist who came to counsel people in their own homes. She said she had used him herself because she had struggled with some issues and he was a great help to her. I said that I would give it a go, no harm done by trying to get some help.

Every week for the next few months I saw this psychiatrist at my home, and he was a great help to me. I have never had any problem being open and sharing my frustrations, so as I was under his counsel I had a lot of questions answered. I suffered from insomnia and I had started having horrible nightmares again, which made me even more depressed. The nightmares were so real that I couldn't separate them from reality, and they left me exhausted. I was able to talk to him about all the recurring nightmares, and he explained to me what they might mean.

One nightmare particularly stood out. In the dream Mum had died but the burial was not going to be held at the cemetery. I dreamt that there was a new custom in the village because they had run out of space to bury their dead. All coffins now had to be pushed out from the seashore and the sea would be their last resting place. I stood on the shore of the fjord seeing a whole crowd of people in black attending Mum's funeral. Dad was wearing his black suit, trying to send Mum's coffin off out to sea. I thought to myself, this is wrong. She needs a proper burial, and she needs to be put in a real grave. As Dad pushed the coffin out, a wave washed it back to shore. This happened several times before he successfully pushed the coffin out to the fjord, and it sailed off.

Suddenly, though, I was on a ferry on the same fjord and I was surrounded by coffins everywhere, but now the coffins had deteriorated, and the lids were open. I saw half deteriorated remains of people everywhere. These images were the same as in the video "Thriller," and as I saw the corpses in their coffins covering the entire fjord, I started to shout, "Where is Mum? Where is Mum? I don't want to see Mum like this! You should have buried her in the ground, not at sea. She should have been buried at the cemetery."

My psychiatrist patiently listened to every detail of this nightmare, and he said it was easy for him to understand what was going on in my subconscious. He explained to me that I had probably not accepted my Mum's death at all and that I kept her alive by ringing the phone at the farm, hoping she would answer. Every morning when I woke up, he said, I had to deal with the same shock as the day I got the news that she was dying.

He explained that the dream of sending Mum's coffin out to sea made it possible for me to bump into her remains at any time. This showed that I had not buried her in the ground where she belonged now, as a dead person. By burying her at sea where she could pop up at any time, the waves of unacceptance would bring her back. I needed to put Mum in the ground, he said, and if I didn't, she would pop up everywhere until I gave her a proper burial. It helped me so much to have things explained to me like that. I made a decision to give Mum a proper burial in my mind and to put her in the ground, and the way I did that was that I accepted she was dead.

The psychiatrist helped me with other dreams. I had another dream that haunted me for a long time. I dreamt that I found myself walking in the hallway downstairs at the farm. Then Mum appeared out of nowhere and came walking slowly towards me. Her appearance had changed; she was very different. Her face was as grey as ashes, and her eyes were empty as if they were without life. She was staring with an empty look into the air. Her lips were dry and swollen, and she smiled vaguely with an expression I had not seen before. It looked like it was Mum standing before me, but I got confused; it was as if she was someone else.

I ran towards her and threw my arms around her. Her body was cold, without warmth at all, and then I grabbed her hands into mine and asked her, "Why have you left me, why didn't you tell me you were leaving and where you were going? Where on earth have you been? You can't just leave me like this for three months and not say where you are. You can't just leave me not knowing if you would come back or not. I thought you were dead; I have been so worried that something bad had happened to you. Mum, you need to tell me where you have been; I need to know. Tell me if you are going back there without saying goodbye again. Please don't leave me again! Things have changed, I now understand. If you are leaving again I need you to please tell me if you are going to a nice place. I need to know you are happy."

I wanted her to answer me and talk to me so I could hear

her voice to make sure it was really Mum. She said, "I am
fine; I have just been away for a while," but when she talked it
wasn't like Mum speaking. It had almost the same sound, but
it wasn't her. Then she took both of my hands and they were
clasped together in her hands. Then suddenly Mum's appearance
changed. Her mouth opened into a large monster, and her tongue
was split on the end like a snake's — she was going to swallow me
into her mouth! Half way into her mouth, I woke up screaming
and soaked in sweat.

Having all sorts of nightmares left me exhausted in the
mornings, and it was so hard to cope when I was trying to be a
mother to my own kids. The psychiatrist explained to me that the
way I was handling Mum's death was consuming my whole life. I
had to refocus on what I was meditating on. I saw how this dream
was relevant to how I was dealing with Mum's death, and I decided
to get on with my life and a life without having a mum.

But the psychiatrist also helped ease the guilt I felt over
Mum's death. Ted had told me just two days after her death that
it was my fault she died, and his words had become engraved
onto my conscience. I had also become obsessed by the thought
that I had no right to live because I had killed Mum. I was getting
more and more obsessed with the thought that the wrong person
was dead — Mum should have lived and I should have died.

When I told the psychiatrist that I felt guilty for leaving her
that morning, just a few days before she died, and how she had
continued to drink, he wisely turned the tables around. "Let's
look at your own children," he said, "and also think about your
own background and everything you have been through. Let's
say you started to seek comfort in alcohol and you became an
alcoholic and were unable to look after yourself properly. If you

happened to die just like your mother, would you like Frank and Miriam to take the blame for that, and for them to be responsible for your life?"

"No way, in a million years," I said. "I would never want my kids to think like that. It's my life, and I am responsible for it, not them." He then said, "Your Mum would never have wanted you to carry any burden for her death either; it was her problem, not yours."

I had never thought of it like that. The way he explained everything to me and put into words the chaos I was feeling on the inside, helped me so much to understand what was going on. He taught me many lessons by putting in order what was out of order in my mind. He showed me that I wasn't responsible for Mum's death. I still regretted that I had left Mum that day as I never saw her again, but the psychiatrist taught me that it wasn't my fault she died. Mum died as a result of years and years of abuse to her own body, eating very little food, and pumping herself full of alcohol and tablets. Even though it all seems very obvious in hindsight, I had been blinded by grief and guilt, which made it impossible for me to think rationally and logically, and I had been unable to get over it without professional help.

Chapter 30

SPLITTING UP

My marriage with Jim was deteriorating rapidly. We were slipping more and more away from each other. I became increasingly jealous when Jim received phone calls at strange times. I also became suspicious when Jim came home after midnight claiming he had been at a very important bank meeting—even though the banks all closed at 4 pm! We ended up arguing a lot, mostly about his never being home. I wanted him to be with me more and also home to help me with the kids. I put all my energy into trying to be a good mother for my children and making my home look nice, but I desperately longed to receive love. On the inside I felt like there was an empty black hole that grew bigger and bigger by the day. All the affection between Jim and I had gone; it seemed like we were just existing together. We were like an old couple, whose romance and love had long gone.

There were, of course, many things that happened between Jim and me that I am unable to write about that played a part in the breakdown of our marriage. I would in no way suggest that this was only Jim's fault. I must have been a very difficult person to live with, with my broken background, and the way I behaved when I felt rejected. I definitely had a problem with anger, and I allowed myself to explode, excusing it because of what I had been through. I justified to myself that I had the right to be like this, I had the right to say what I felt, I had the right to burst out with every feeling because I was mistreated and rejected as a child. I was like this because what others had done to me. I was totally drowning in self pity and everything was everybody else's fault.

I felt that Jim and I had totally slipped apart from each other and it had gone so far that I didn't even like Jim anymore after things that had happened between us. In the end I went so cold that I didn't even care about him anymore. I knew he had fallen out of love with me and that I didn't love him anymore either.

*****

After Mum's death I started to visit Auntie Wilma up north again. Jim was never around and I didn't mind spending my holidays alone with the kids. I didn't like to visit the farm much after what Dad said at the funeral. So I took Frank and Miriam on holiday and spent several weeks at Wilma's in the summer of 1987. Almost every evening after I had put the kids to bed, Wilma put her homemade spirit on the table and we sat and drank a few drinks before we got tipsy. Wilma is hilarious and can crack jokes like no one I know. It was so fun to be around her, and we would sit there and laugh about everything and nothing, almost wetting our knickers about the crazy stuff that came of her mouth.

Since I had loads of friends up north from my childhood trips, it was great to be around well known friends. I also started to go out to the nightclub in town three times a week; it was open on Wednesdays, Fridays, and Saturdays. I usually left the house around 9 pm when the kids had been sleeping since 8, and I stayed out and partied till around 4 am, just enough time to get back home for a couple of hours sleep before they woke up.

During my three weeks stay up north I met a very charming guy who always asked me to dance with him at the nightclub, and I loved to dance. He gave me lovely compliments and I was drinking it all in like sweet songs for my soul. The empty hole with lack of love on the inside, felt like it was slowly being filled with sweetness, and a bubbling feeling started to grow. This man knew exactly how to wrap a woman around his little finger. Sadly, I didn't know at that time that he was the biggest flirt in town, but I was so naive that I truly went for it. I was starved for attention, so I was gladly drinking in every drop of it.

Eventually it got to the point that I followed him home one night, and we, of course, ended up kissing, but I didn't want go further. In the back of my head I was thinking, "I can't, I can't, I am married." But I sure did fall in love with him. I had not had attention like that for many years, and he ignited something inside me that I forgot existed. This man also made me feel attractive, and I had not felt attractive for a long time either. Fairytales have an end, though, and eventually the summer was over and I had to go back home to Jim. I was unable to think about anything other than this man I had met. One thing was sure—I had lost all interest in Jim.

The year went by and Jim and I were back in our normal routine, but I had changed on the inside. I was still at home looking after the kids and Jim came home late every evening. When there were parties on the street at our estate I was wild and crazy, flirting with everyone. My skirts went shorter and shorter and the cuts on the chest went lower and lower. I was soon looking forward to going back up north to visit Wilma again; I simply could not wait. Will I see this man I had been thinking about for a whole year? By now I was totally put off by Jim; my heart belonged to this other man and I didn't care. This man had made me feel like a woman.

When I went on holiday the following summer in 1988, I spent several weeks up north and loved every minute of it. I went out to the disco three times a week as I did the previous year, and I spent time with the man I had fallen in love with. I loved it because he didn't drink and he could take me home after the party, but first we went to his place and I stayed there till the early morning hours. This time I didn't care that I was married anymore. I decided that when I would go back home I would ask Jim for a divorce. With those thoughts going on in my mind I slept with this man during my holiday; in my head I was already divorced.

Eventually my "cloud 9" summer holiday was over, back to the grey days of monotony. Jim picked me and the kids up from the airport and I didn't say much to him in the car; I felt very depressed leaving the man I had fallen in love with. I wanted to pick the right opportunity to tell Jim I wanted out of the marriage. There was so much to do when I arrived home and I had to get the kids to bed, the time had gone, and I still had not been able to find an opportunity to tell Jim I wanted a divorce. Eventually we went to bed; Jim approached me indicating he wanted sex. It was so long since we had slept together that I had forgotten the last time Jim approached me like that. I would never have thought he would want anything like that from me since our relationship was down the drain. When Jim approached me I simply didn't dare to stop him. I had not managed to pluck up enough courage to tell Jim I wanted a divorce, and this had now become totally awkward. I suddenly felt guilty over what I had done on holiday. I felt sorry for Jim because I knew he was a good man, even though I didn't love him anymore, and I was now in love with someone else.

As an act of obligation I let Jim sleep with me. I was in a total dilemma; I did not want to sleep with him at all because I felt I committed adultery against this other man that I was so in love with. After sleeping with Jim, it made it harder to pluck up the courage to say I wanted a divorce. I simply could not do it. The rehearsal of my divorce speech in my mind had sounded so easy, but to actually pluck up the courage to do so face to face was very hard. One day merged into another and I was totally stuck about how to do it; the right opportunity never seemed to come.

It didn't make matters any better when after a few weeks I suddenly felt sick when the aroma of coffee filled the room. I had always been addicted to my lovely morning coffee, but suddenly I was almost vomiting at a tiny smell of it. I knew exactly what that sign meant. I knew I was pregnant. I was totally devastated. Another child! I was 22 years old and pregnant with my third kid. The biggest problem I faced was that I had no idea who was the father of the child I was carrying. There was no way I could even think of having an abortion. That was totally out of the question because I had always had strong opinions against it.

A few days later I went to the doctor to confirm my suspicions and found out I was pregnant. As I was driving back home I cried so hard that I was almost unable to see where I was driving. I drove past a big cliff and I wanted to crash my car into it to commit suicide, but I could not stand the thought that I would kill my unborn baby at the same time. Although my driving was erratic, I managed to keep the car on the road until I got home.

I cried and cried for days, I was so afraid. "Who is the dad of my child?" Thoughts began echoing from my past: "Who am I? Who do I belong to? Who is my dad? If dad is not my dad, what is a whore child? Have I produced a whore child?"

And how on earth could I ask for a divorce, now that I was pregnant? There would be no way for me to be able to cope alone. Throughout the whole of my pregnancy I was in great stress because I didn't know who the father of my child was. Will my child suffer? Will my child be rejected like I was? These were the thoughts that went through my head all the time. Voices from the past haunted me: "Bastard, you are illegitimate, you are a whore child, you don't belong here." Will the child that I was carrying in my belly experience the same as I did as a kid? I was terrified that I was now producing a "whore child." Am I passing on the curse that is on my life to this poor innocent child? I was tormented day and night and terrified of what would happen to the child that I was going to give birth to. There was only one thing I was certain of, no matter how bad I felt the situation was, abortion was totally out of the question. This child had been conceived and it had a right to live, no matter who the father was.

My pregnancy was totally horrendous. My back had hurt during the pregnancies of my other children, but during this one I could hardly walk. My pelvis had become so slack, that the pain was horrific. At only two months pregnant I got a disabled badge in my car so that I could park near the shops. I could not even turn myself around in bed when I was sleeping; I was totally helpless.

My marriage to Jim was getting worse every day. I was constantly pleading with him to come home earlier to help me with the kids because I was unable to do even the simplest of chores. Making dinner, I had to sit on a tall chair whilst I was preparing it. I was unable to lift anything heavy. I would walk slowly across the room and suddenly my legs couldn't hold me up and I would fall down on my knees. There was nothing the doctors could do for my condition. They said it was normal that the pelvis got worse after each pregnancy.

On May the 9th 1989 my youngest son Joel was born. The labour went well and a big healthy boy was placed in my arms. I looked at my son's face and it was not like either of my other two kids. A knife pierced my heart. I haven't even heard from the guy up north that I had fallen so much in love with. I waved the thought away as soon as it entered my head as I didn't want to even think about it at all. All I kept thinking were thoughts like, "I don't care, this is MY son, and I love him and that is the only thing that counts right now".

A year later, in the spring, I told Jim I wanted a divorce. He agreed and we went to a lawyer together and signed the papers for separation. We also agreed on how to share our properties. Jim kept the flat and I kept the house we owned. Then I took out a mortgage and paid him a lump sum to make up the difference because the house was worth more than the flat. On the way home from the lawyer's office, I totally broke down in the car crying; I was so sad that my life had turned out the way it did. I had loved Jim once and now it was all over. All of our shared memories and history were over. At the age of 24 I was divorced and entered a new season as a single mother: Frank was five, Miriam was four, and Joel was one year old.

Chapter 31

"TAKE THE TABLETS"

After a few weeks I felt very happy to be alone. I didn't have to wait for someone that was almost never at home and was always late. I went out partying now and again and loved all the attention I got from men at the parties. The summer went fast and I had a great time being free and single, just flirting with life. I felt like a rose coming into full blossom.

When autumn arrived Jim had difficulties seeing the children where he lived and he told me that the only way he was able to spend time with them was if he stayed at the house. He couldn't move into the flat that he had taken over until the tenants had moved out. I was starting to get more and more mentally and physically exhausted with having no help with the kids. I agreed that Jim could come home every second weekend to spend it at the house with the kids.

For a while Jim came and went as we agreed, every second weekend, and he was always great with the kids. I used to spend those weekends visiting my sister's homes. But after a while it was difficult to find a place to stay when Jim was at the house. I ended up staying at home when Jim was there, and it turned out great. We even started to have normal conversations with each other. I started to look forward to Jim coming home and I missed him when he went. We never used to have great times together when we were married—this was so strange! I started to regret that I had wanted a divorce and began thinking we should not have split up at all. We could have made it work. It seemed like Jim liked it too, being the family father from Fridays to Sundays, then leaving the house into freedom for two whole weeks before he came back playing the same role again. But the situation was starting to take its toll on me. Going through the trauma that a divorce brings and yet still living almost like a normal family for a few days a month was very confusing. I began more and more to live in denial and was quickly sinking into the deep darkness of depression.

I would go to bed and pray to a God the same prayer I always prayed and ask if he existed. I asked if He could show me if He was out there. I was praying to Him to send me signs from heaven to show me there was a God. I used to ask that He let three stars fall from the sky, then I would know he was there. I often opened my curtains to see the pitch black sky full of shining stars and hoped the stars would fall so I could know that there was a God out there, but nothing happened. I waited and waited and on occasion I saw one or two meteors fall burning through the sky, but the third one never came.

My sleep was bad; I still had nightmares that were haunting me. I became exhausted from lack of sleep. I had tried very hard for a long time to cope with it all and not to cry. I was afraid that if I let myself go, I would lose it completely. I kept holding back the best I could, but one day I felt so down that I started to sob. I cried so hard that I could not stop. I went into my bathroom to try and wash the tears off my face, to try to stop them from flowing.

But unable to stop crying I just fell down on the cold bathroom floor, curling up in a foetal position, and I just cried and cried. In the end I was crying hysterically, followed by hyperventilating.

It felt like a dark cloud was covering me all over. I felt as though I was trapped in a dark cloud, unable to get out, unable to let anyone in. Laying on the floor, staring into nothing, I was transported back in time. All the emotions of every bad thing that had ever happened to me since I was a little girl came back in full force and surrounded me with pain. I felt like all the air had been knocked out of me at once; I don't know how long I was lying on the bathroom floor, but I became again the little girl that had just been beaten and was lost. Still in a foetal position, I started rocking my head on the hard lino back and forth, back and forth, just as I used to do so many years before, when my world was spinning. Thankfully my kids were not at home at that time so they didn't see me like that.

There were also evenings when I was getting my kids ready for bed and I would be very near breaking point. I would sink onto one of their beds while they were still in the bathroom and cry. When the kids came into the bedroom I was not able to explain to them what was wrong with their mum, because I didn't know myself at the time what was happening to me. When the kids came in and found their mother crying on one of their beds, they tried to comfort me the best they could. When they asked me why I was crying, I told them I was just tired, there is nothing to worry about. Sadly, I was unable to protect them from seeing the misery I was in then.

I realized I needed help and I went to see the doctor concerning my sleep. The doctor finally persuaded me to take sleeping tablets. I was scared to receive the sleeping tablets, because I had seen what tablets had done to Mum, but I thought to myself, I have to try it even if it is for a couple of days, just to get some rest. I thought, I will just take them when I am really desperate. I never told the doctor how depressed I was feeling and how I felt I could not cope.

I handed in my prescription at the pharmacy and received three boxes of sleeping tablets that should keep me sleeping for three months. I tried the tablets for a few days, but they only left me more tired. I yawned throughout the whole day, and I still didn't feel rested. The heaviness that was weighing me down all the time became heavier and heavier as my thoughts transported me back to my childhood and also it left me feeling like a failure.

I began to think the world would be a better place without people like me. I had put away the sleeping tablets in my night table because they were starting to shout out loud that I had to take all of them in one go. I wanted to escape from the pain I was feeling on the inside. The thoughts I had from my past were ringing in my head: "I've got to get away; I've got to get away." Then the thoughts became stronger: "Take all the tablets, then you will get rest and peace, the kids don't need you, nobody needs you, you need to be dead, and that is what you deserve. Your only solution is ending your life; how else do you think you can get rid of the pain?"

I was trapped in this black bubble where my mind was bombarded with destructive thoughts. For many weeks I meditated on those thoughts until they finally convinced me that there was no other way out for me than to end my life. I made a decision to do so one weekend when Jim came to pick up the kids. He had finally found a temporary place to stay until the flat became available.

Jim was going to pick up the kids the following day and I had prepared to exit into eternity once he picked up the kids. I didn't want to write a suicide letter; I had nothing to say to anyone. All I was thinking of was death and nothing else. I had bought a couple of beers, I knew the combination of alcohol and tablets would have a quick effect, and that I would not feel anything if I used the beer to swallow all the tablets.

I went to bed, and on what I was thinking would be my last night alive, I once more opened the curtains of my bedroom window to see the stars. I started to ask if there was a God out there. I said, "Please, God, GIVE ME A SIGN. Please let three stars fall so I can know if there is something out there, please! If there is a God out there give me this sign." I waited and waited and nothing happened. Then I had an idea. I had a Bible in my night table drawer. I had read some of it before but I was unable to understand what I was reading. I was thinking, "Maybe the 'God' that the Bible talks about will give me a sign if I read in that book. This is my last chance to find out if he is out there since it is my last night alive."

I was scared of death even when I wanted it so much. Then I opened the book randomly and stuck my finger on a place and started to read from there. The reason why I am quoting what I read that night is because it seemed like a blueprint of my life. My finger landed on Hosea, chapter 2, and I read from verses 1 to 13. I am quoting verses 1 to 7 from the Norwegian translation of 1978 which says this:

Carry complaint against their mother,
carry complaints against her!
Because she is not my wife,
and I am not her husband.

Let her remove the look of a whore
from her face
and the mark of a whore away from her breasts!
If not, I will dress her naked
and put her on display as
the day she was born.
I will let her become like a desert
Make her like a dry land
and let her die of thirst.
Her children I will show no mercy
because they are whore children.
Because their mother was unfaithful,
the one who gave birth to them
did shameful acts.

She said:

I will run after my lovers,
that gives me bread and water,
wool and linen, oil and vine.
Look, therefore I will shut
the way for her with thorns.
I will build a brick wall in front of her,
so that she will not find her ways.
Now she is running after her lovers,
she will not find them,
when she looks for them,
she will be unable to find them.
Then she will say:
I want to return to my first husband,
because I was happier
then than now.

As I read those horrendous judgemental words, tears were flowing down my face. All the 13 verses were directly pointing the finger at me. As I continued to read down to verse 13, I could not bear it any longer. I threw the Bible at the wall and cried and cried. There it was again, "WHORE," the well known word that I had grown up hearing. I was a "whore child" and my children were "whore children".

I knew that if there was a God out there, there was no way He wanted me. I was a whore child in His eyes too, just like I had been in Dad's eyes. I was just too bad and filthy a person for God to want. I had sought God as a last chance to help me, just like I had done when I was eight years old and was on my way to the snow-covered road to kill myself. I asked God to save me then and he didn't; I asked God now to show himself to me, and he didn't. Instead of seeing God, I just saw my ugly self.

I finally went to sleep and woke up next morning to prepare for my kids to be picked up by Jim in the afternoon. I had it all figured out; I'd decided in what order I was going to take the tablets. All the bags were packed for the kids, the beer was ready in the fridge, I had emptied all the tablets into a cup and I put them on the top of the fridge. As the hours went by I was so obsessed with the thought that I had to take the tablets that I was not scared any longer. All I could think of was the tablets. I didn't think of how the kids would react or how it would be for them not to have a mother, and I didn't think what effect it would have on them later in life knowing their mother had committed suicide. I had only one thought in my head, "Get it over with." I felt I had to hurry.

Jim came and the kids were excited to see him. I didn't give them any longer goodbyes than normal; I could not wait till they were out of the door so that I could just end my life. Jim got the kids in the car and came back and picked up their bags. I had taken a handful of tablets just as he arrived. I didn't want to get cold feet once they had gone so I had taken just a few and swallowed them with the beer. Once he went out of the door to leave, I ran back into the kitchen and took the rest of the tablets and drank a ½ pint of beer to get them down. I went into my living room and sat down on my settee waiting for it all to be over. That's the last thing I remember.

*****

I opened my eyes and there was a big clock on the wall in front of me; it was exactly 12 o'clock. I didn't know if it was day or night. I don't remember much. But I couldn't understand why there would be a clock in death. The walls around me were pale yellow and I found myself in a bed in a corridor. I suddenly realized that I was not dead, I was in the hospital. It was very quiet. I saw no people, then I turned my head around and there was Jim sitting on a chair by the bed.

I felt shame and embarrassment fill every part of my consciousness. I had failed to kill myself, and now they know. I felt I had sunk below my lowest point. I also remember that there was something about the time on the clock; superstitious as I was, I believed it meant something. I made a decision that I will never in my whole life allow myself to sink so low.

Then I panicked. I got out of bed and I said again and again, "I've got to get out of here, I've got to get away, I don't belong here, and I've got to get out." All I could think of was that I needed to disappear, I needed to escape, I needed to be alone. I was confused about why death didn't work, why was I still here, what went wrong? I only remember small details, I remember signing some papers before I wobbled down the corridor to leave the hospital, I remember cold air hitting my face as I went outside, and the next thing I remember was that I was laying in my own bed at home. For the next few days I don't remember much because of the effect of the tablets. I do remember I tried to drink coffee and I remember spilling it all over me. I was too ashamed to ask how I got to the hospital, but apparently when I thought Jim had left he was still outside. He came back into the house to pick up the last bag of the kids' clothes which he'd forgotten about.

After that event I slowly got on with my life. I didn't think about death anymore; I had tried that, and it didn't work. The first thing I saw when I woke up from the suicide attempt was the clock showing 12 midnight; in my superstitious mind I thought it must have meant something. I thought of it as a sign, my life was not meant to be over. I was stuck with being alive and had to make the best out of it. I was only 24 ½ years old and I had to wait and see what life would bring.

Chapter 32

SEARCHING FOR LOVE

I decided that if I was going to live this life, I would truly live it to the maximum. From now on I would try to make the best of it. I would choose to have fun and I would get out of the house more. For the next two and a half years I threw myself into the world of parties. Whenever I managed to find babysitters, I enjoyed whatever the nightclubs had to offer. I decided that was the way to live life. I was not going to sit at home and suffer or become like a nun and bore myself to death. I also wanted to have attention and I wanted to have loads of it.

The partying was great fun to begin with, but then I started to get involved in relationships with men. I was starved for attention and it led me, in the beginning, to use them to get attention. It was a great feeling to be wanted and to show them who was in charge. I dated guy after guy. I was playing the "game", but in doing so I was also crushing their hearts.

I didn't care though; I had been hurt by men before, and now it was their turn. I had never forgotten what had happened to me when I was 15, and Steven had forced himself on me. I don't know if wanting revenge was playing in my subconscious, but it may have been one of the reasons I was behaving so badly towards men.

Partying was exciting to begin with, but after a while it left me feeling even emptier than before. I knew how to wrap a man around my little finger and I knew every trick in the flirting game. But at the end of the day, I felt like I was left with a big black hole in my heart that grew bigger and bigger. The more I gave away of me, the more I felt like pieces of me were gone. I longed for someone to love and who could love me with true love.

I was still haunted by my past, reliving traumas that I had been through. I often fell down in a ditch of self pity, feeling very sorry for myself from the stolen years of my childhood. When the parties were over, the music had stopped, and I was alone in my bed, I would pull back the curtains and look at the stars, and ask again if there was a God out there. I would often wet my pillow with tears and cry myself to sleep praying, "God help me, God show yourself to me. If you are there, let three stars fall, then I will know you are there."

After a while I also started to get involved in serious relationships which I thought was love, but they never seemed to work out. Then the way I tried to try to forget one man was to get involved with another one. But, sadly, I fell in love with the other man, too, and that didn't work out either, and so on it went. I so much wanted to be loved and I wanted to find someone who could love me for who I was, and not because he wanted sex and not just because he found me attractive. But I never found a man like that in the places I was looking.

Midweek I was always at home. I could not go anywhere because of the kids. I didn't mind; I had always loads to do. I had lots of contact with my cousin Ken; he lived on the same estate as me. We often used to sit up till 2-3 in the morning playing cards and drinking "Jeagermaister". We didn't get drunk, but we laughed and enjoyed ourselves with the card games and I also practised my fortune telling on him.

Auntie Wilma had moved to the Canary Islands and I went to visit her a few times. There I got involved in a relationship, too. But down on the islands there's nothing to do but party every day. I had become scared of turning into an alcoholic so I found a solution. I decided I would start to drink "Cerveca sin alcohol" - non alcoholic beer while I was visiting the island. I was excited that Wilma had moved down there, and I also wanted to take my kids and move there too. I had fallen in love with the island and also a local man that lived the party life there. I was convinced that the lifestyle of partying would fit me well. I loved the sea and the palm trees, not to mention the weather. I thought the kids would of course be okay, with a Norwegian school on the island.

I was 26 years old and had travelled a lot of times to visit Wilma at the Canaries. During the autumn of 1992 I decided to make plans to leave Norway and move to the island and continue to party with this "party animal" I was dating. I had to wait till my kids finished their term in school the following summer. I was so excited about the new future that I was going to build, I could hardly wait till summer. I had people coming to view my house, which I was going to let out for a year. My plans were fixed, or so I thought.

On New Year's Eve of 1992, my sister Sally invited me and the kids to celebrate the evening with her. We enjoyed a lovely meal together. Then everyone got ready for the traditional fireworks that would start at 12 midnight. At five to 12 we went outside in the freezing cold night. The ground was covered with thick snow, and it was very beautiful. I went out onto my sister's balcony to view the fireworks, while Frank, Miriam and Joel went with Sally and her kids down into the garden where they were lighting the fireworks.

In just a few moments, the black sky exploded with lovely sparkling colours; one after the other fireworks went off in big bangs. The spectacular colour display in the sky lasted for about 15-20 minutes. The temperature outside was about -15 C, and I became too cold to stand on the balcony until the firework show was over, so I went back into the warm living room. As I walked across the floor my eyes glanced at the clock on the wall; it still said 12 midnight. I thought, "That's strange; it was 5 to 12 when I went outside and the time on my watch says 12:15." I hesitated. 12 midnight. My superstition kicked in. It must mean something. I'd always thought that strange things like that had to be a sign. And to me the number 12 was no ordinary number. There was something magical about it. I remembered the clock at the hospital two and a half years earlier, it had also shown 12. Because of this magic number, I made a decision then not to ever sink so low again and I made up my mind to change my life into a more positive one.

I sat down on the couch and stared at the clock on the wall — 12 midnight. At this moment I became convinced that the clock had stopped for a reason. Then a weird thought rushed through my head, "This is going to be the summer of all summers, and you are not going to move to the Canaries, you are going to stay in Norway." The thought sounded so loud in my head that it almost rang like church bells. In one moment my plans changed. I made an instant decision to follow the strong feeling inside.

I knew that there was no way I could go to the Canaries now.

Stolen Childhood

The green light that had been there before saying "Go" had now become a big red light flashing, "Don't go! Don't go!" The urge to stay and wait for what would happen in the summer settled it for me. I felt like I had just had a sign. I had no idea where it came from, but I knew I had to stay in Norway. I also became very excited about what the summer was going to bring. "The summer of all summers," I thought to myself, "that sounds absolutely fantastic. I wonder if I am going to meet someone here in Norway, maybe some 'hunk' of a man."

Chapter 33

A NEW BEGINNING

I rang Wilma the next day and told her that I had changed my mind about and living in the Canaries. She told me it was probably the best for me and the kids to stay in Norway. She said she had been a little bit worried about the kids living there. "There is so much drinking here and you rarely see a sober person," she said. She had been worried that the lifestyle there would get me into trouble and would kill me in the end.

About two months later in February of 1993 I went again to visit Wilma; I took the kids with me on holiday. It was in the half term holiday and we had a great time. I always used to sunbathe topless, only wearing a small thong, I didn't care. I just wanted as few white marks as possible on my body. But this time I stayed in a two bedroom apartment in a quiet area with no party people around.

I came home and after a couple of weeks the kids went to stay with Jim for the weekend. I was bored after being away on holiday and I drove to the city to go to the cinema to see if I could put my mind on things other than the palm trees and the lovely sun that I had enjoyed. It was very rare I went to the city, but it was a lovely warm winter day beginning of March and the snow had melted from the streets and there was almost spring in the air.

I didn't expect the movie to be such a rollercoaster ride of emotions. I watched the movie "Alive," a true story about an air crash in the Andes, and the people who survived for 72 days in the mountains. They survived the air crash, avalanches and starvation for all that time, and they even started to eat the bodies of the dead people to keep themselves alive.

During one scene in the movie I could not hold back my tears. It was about one of the men who was trying to find a way out, to find help. After reaching one of the mountaintops and still seeing endless chains of mountains covered in snow, the actor said, "It's impossible, we have survived all this. It's impossible, it's impossible. It's beautiful. It's wonderful. Can you feel God? He is all over, He is everywhere, God is everywhere."

When the actor said those words, I was touched to the core of my heart. I began crying and I also got the chills. I had been very warm when I went into the cinema, but was now freezing cold; I had to put my coat back on. The movie became very real to me; it was like I was there together with the people on the mountain. I watched those people survive in unbearably cold conditions on top of a mountain after an airplane wreck. I thought, "It's true, it is impossible for them to survive all that, avalanches, starvation, and the cold." Watching the movie made me realize that it was impossible for me to have survived what I had endured without there being a God. It must have been God that had kept me alive.

I had a problem though, I didn't know who God was, and I didn't know where he was. I really wanted to know, but I didn't know where to start to look for God, I had no idea where to find Him.

A few weeks later I started to get telephone calls from Wilma's youngest son Rick. He was the twin's little brother. Rick and I had conversations on the phone that lasted for two to three hours. We were always on the phone after the kids were put to bed. Sometimes we would talk till 3 in the morning, even though Rick had to get up for work at 6 am. I don't know how he survived on so little sleep.

Rick had become a Christian a few years earlier, and he was one of those people that called themselves "saved". I thought it was strange to call yourself "saved" and I felt uncomfortable about that word—it sounded so "Christian," and so weird. I didn't like the word "Christian" either, it sounded "super holy" and boring. I thought that people who said they were Christian thought they were better than the rest of us. And the Christians I had seen were weird.

My perception of a Christian woman was that she never wore makeup, she always wore unfashionable grey and boring clothes that made her look like a "cow." Her hair would be tied back in a knot at the back with a middle parting as wide as the Grand Canyon, and she would have big, bushy, unplucked eyebrows and wear a pair of ugly round glasses that would rest on the tip of her nose. Her mouth would be difficult to separate from the rest of her face because it would be so tightly squeezed and would make her lips white and cracked. She would also be hitting people over the head with a stick, just like a teacher from the 1800's, if they disagreed with her. I definitely didn't want to be a Christian woman.

I kept asking Rick what he knew about God, and I tried the best I could to debate him into a corner when he talked to me about his God. "Why are people starving? Why do babies die?

Why are people abused? Why is there such difference between rich and poor? Why doesn't God stop it, if he is almighty and if he is God? If there is a devil, why doesn't God just kick his arse and finish him off?"

No matter what I said to Rick he always seemed to make sense of all my chaotic thoughts and questions. He told me later that whenever he had been talking on the phone to me, he had a Bible on his lap, and he used to just sit and read from it, when I asked him all those questions. I was totally amazed how he responded, and sometimes Rick even honestly said that he didn't know the answer to this and that. I liked that he was honest and told me that he didn't know everything.

After several weeks of conversation, Rick put me in a corner with our conversation. He said to me, "Laila, why don't you receive God now?"

"What do you mean, 'receive God'?" I asked. "I want to meet him if he is out there somewhere, but I don't know if he is."

"Do you believe in Jesus?" Rick asked.

"Jesus was probably a bloke that walked on the earth a long time ago," I answered. "I know we have the calendar and days after him. Yes, I believe the 'dude Jesus' has been here, but what does Jesus have to do with it?"

Rick said, "If you receive Jesus into your heart you will meet God."

"Receive what in my heart? What do you mean? How can I open my heart without surgery?"

Rick said, "If you believe in your heart that Jesus is Lord and confess him with your mouth, you will be saved."

"Rick, I don't want to get saved or to become a Christian. I know I have done too many bad things to be a Christian. I know if I only lift my thumb I am sinning. I only want God if he is there, if he exists. Can't I just have Him?"

"Yes, you can have God, but you have to receive Jesus into your heart. You see, it is Jesus that will take away your sins. He went to the cross and took the punishment that you and I deserve, so we can stand before God without sin. I will help you and pray with you, then a miracle will take place."

I started laughing my head off, and I said to Rick, "You and me pray here on the phone? That's crazy; prayer is something one does in private."

There was no way I dared to pray with Rick on the phone. He was my cousin, six years younger than me. To pray with him would be far too embarrassing.

Then Rick said, "Laila, what do you have to lose? I know you want God, you have said so and I can help you so you can get to know him. God has already answered your prayer by you and me talking on the phone for so many weeks about Him. God has shown himself to you through me."

A thought from the past slammed into my head. It was almost like a voice loudly speaking in my head saying, "Maybe this is the sign I asked for the day before I tried to commit suicide three years ago."

I said to Rick, "Okay, I will pray with you and receive God. You are right, I want to know Him, but remember this, I do not want to become a 'Christian' and I do not want to become 'saved'. I also want to continue with my parties and I want to continue to have a pint of lager now and again, and I will never change my style of clothes and I will certainly not become a nun."

I heard Rick laughing on the other end of the phone. "Okay, no problem. Do all that if you want, but if you are out at one of your parties and doing all sorts of stuff, you might hear a little voice inside of you telling you other things, and that might be God speaking to you."

"Okay, deal, I am in, let me get God now."

In my superstitious way of thinking I thought we were going to say a magic "formula" and God would appear in my living room, like the genie in Aladdin's lamp. I expected this "fellow God" to show up in front of me. If there was a God out there, this was his chance. I sure wanted him, and if this was the way to find him, I sure didn't mind involving Jesus in it if that was necessary. I had asked long enough if God was there and I now hoped that I could find him this way.

Rick said I should pray the words he said, and repeat them after him: "Dear God, I believe that Jesus is your son. I ask you to forgive me for my sins, and I ask you to come and live in my life now, and I ask you to become my Lord and Saviour, Amen."

As I repeated those words, I felt a huge weight lift off my shoulders, like I had become 200 kilos lighter. I also felt that there was a healing taking place in my body, almost like my blood was cleansed from something bad; relief just flowed through my whole body. God didn't appear in my living room as I had expected, but after praying and meaning those words, I knew that God was there. It was no longer just a "hope" but now I knew that I knew that I knew that God was real and I had found Him.

It was as if a light had been switched on inside my chest and in my mind. I could see clearly, not with my natural eyes, but with the eyes of my guts. God was there and he had come to me. I didn't need to wonder any longer if God was there; now I knew, and I knew for sure.

I didn't understand anything about the miracle that had just taken place or how it had happened; I just had a peace that I cannot explain in words. It was peace with God and all I know is that it felt fantastic.

But the next few days were horrendous. I cried over the smallest little thing. I would go about my normal business and then I would either hurt my head on a cupboard door or my foot would slam into the coffee table and I would swear like an old man down at the docks, just like I always had when I'd hurt myself before. But this time I ended up crying, thinking that God would not want me anymore, now that he heard that I was swearing so much.

Five days later I rang Rick and I told him that I could not take it any longer. I told him that I was crying all the time and I was sure God was angry with me because of my very bad language. I told Rick he had to reverse the "magic" prayer we prayed five days earlier, so I could go back to normal; the emotions were too much for me to handle.

Rick laughed, "Reverse the prayer? That is impossible; you are a child of God now. God is not angry with you just because you swear. I will give you an illustration so you can understand a little bit about how wonderful God is. Imagine when your son Frank was small and he was learning to walk. Imagine Frank taking his first few steps around the coffee table and then he suddenly wobbled and fell down on the floor. On the way down he grabbed the tablecloth that caused the vase to fall and break into many pieces. There would have been a lot of mess everywhere.

"You being his mother would stop whatever you were doing and run to your son who was crying. Then you would pick him up into your arms and comfort him and wipe away his tears. When you had finished hugging him and comforting him and your son had stopped crying, you would put him back down on the floor. The next thing you would do is run to the phone and call all the grandparents and tell them that your son had been so brave today taking his first step. You would not mention at all him falling down or that he broke the vase; all you would do is boast about how brave Frank was that he had taken his first few steps, and you were so proud of him.

"If you can imagine yourself doing that to your own son, then imagine a million times more how much God would do that for us and how proud He is of us when we are learning to walk, when we are daring to take our first steps in our faith. You see, Laila, when you have a baby, it is impossible for the baby to walk when it has only just been born, it takes time to learn. It also takes time for the baby to start eating solid foods. You can only give the baby milk for the first few months, and you can never give a newborn baby a piece of steak. Laila, you have been born again into God's family, and you are just like a little new born child learning to walk. You will grow and learn every day, so don't worry about God getting angry with you. He can't. He loves you too much, so just relax and don't worry. I will send you some teaching tapes that you can listen to that will help you."

I was so relieved when I heard what Rick had just explained to me and I understood what he meant. I knew that God was perfect and I was not, and if I as a mum was gracious when my child fell, I learned that God would be much more gracious than me because he was God and I was not.

*****

There were so many things that happened during the next few

months after I had asked God to come into my life and I received Jesus Christ as Lord and Saviour. Some of the big changes appeared with what I was wearing. The very short revealing skirts and my g string knickers of lace, a dress code that didn't leave much to the imagination, changed gradually. I always used to dress based on how I would feel that day. Would it be glitter or plain black, or would it be a totally see through top with just a lace bra? I would stand in front of the mirror with my "normal" clothes on, trying to get ready to go out shopping or so on. Once I dressed with what I would normally wear, I felt totally naked. I thought that if I go out like this, everyone would see my private parts. Suddenly it mattered to me to cover up. I was desperate; suddenly I could see what I had been revealing. I had never seen before that I had almost gone around totally naked!

Over a period of time, it turned out that I didn't feel comfortable in any of my party clothes either; it was the weirdest thing I have experienced in my life. I used to love those clothes, but now I felt awful that I had ever worn them. It was as if they belonged to someone else, a girl I could not relate to any longer. I had a huge problem. I hardly had any decent clothes at all, and my whole wardrobe contained revealing and see-through items. The pop singer Cher and I used to have the same taste for clothes; we both wore strings of fabric to cover up as little as possible.

I didn't have much money to buy new clothes but over a period of time, my mini skirts became longer and longer and my tops became less and less revealing. I had not yet read the Bible, neither had I been to any church. The changes in me came from the inside out. I wasn't told to change by anyone.

I kept in contact with Rick on the phone and I asked him more questions than ever. He started to send me audio tapes with teaching from the Bible. The first tape he sent me was teaching about "youth, love and sex." I loved all of it and I thought that everyone that visited me would also love it, too. Whenever someone came visiting me I ran to my stereo and put on the Bible teaching tapes so my guests could hear this wonderful news. I would jump up from my sofa and shout with joy, saying to my friends, "This is absolutely fantastic, this is from the Bible, can you believe it? The Bible talks about sex, it's not old fashioned at all. This is the type of love I have been trying to find all these years, can you believe it? One man and one woman. Not many men and many women, but only one man that would love me. God made Adam and Eve not Adam and Eve and Becky, Linda and Mary. God didn't make Eve and Adam, then John then Ben then Chris. God only made the two first, Adam and Eve, it's only meant to be two. That is how God created us from the beginning. It's fantastic we are not meant to go after one then another. That is the reason why we are not happy, we are meant to be with only one. Wow! It all makes sense, a man that would only have one woman and a woman that would only have one man, no cheating on each other."

My friends had a different opinion of the tapes I put on. They would listen politely for a while, but in the end they asked me to please switch the tapes off. I could not understand why they didn't find them as thrilling as I did. I thought to myself that the whole world needs to hear this teaching. It's fantastic and it is freeing to hear it.

One night when I was on the phone to Rick, he told me that I needed to find a church. He said it was so important to be in a church so that I could grow in God. I told Rick I didn't want to be involved in any cults and silly churches. I told him that I had been to the Lutheran church on the 17th of May, just three days after we had prayed together. I wanted to hear what the priest had to say about God. My ears were ready to hear; they were as big as saucepan lids. I was very disappointed because the priest didn't talk about God at all; he had only talked about how great it was to see so many people in the church on our Constitution Day. I thought it was silly of the priest to say such a thing because it was obvious that there would be many in church on Constitution Day. All the school children had to go.

The priest also talked about the trees that were getting green and the life that was budding. I thought to myself that you had to be a fool if you didn't know that spring had arrived, everyone knew that. I had become very irritated because the priest didn't tell the people what many of them probably didn't know, that God really existed and that He was here and everyone that wanted him could have him in their life. Why didn't the priest tell the whole church, that they could just pray a simple prayer to receive Jesus who could help them like Rick had helped me? Then the whole church would get to know God. I had wanted to jump up from the pews in the church and shout to them this wonderful news that I had just learned about myself. With great difficulty, I zipped my lips.

I told Rick that going to church was not for me. I can be with God on my own, I said. I didn't want any priest to waste my time. I said that I only wanted to continue to listen to what was on the teaching tapes and asked him if he could send me some more of those. Rick told me that he knew of a church that was totally different from the church that I had been to on the 17th of May and it was not too far from where I lived. Rick told me that in that church they taught in exactly the same way as they did on those tapes he had been sending to me. I told Rick that I would love to go to a place to hear live what I had been hearing on the tapes, but I would never dare to go alone. Rick offered to come and take me to the church that he thought would be perfect for me and where he thought I would feel at home.

Although Rick lived about 90 miles away from me, he drove up one week to visit me and take me to that church. It had been over a month since the night I had prayed with Rick, and I found myself for the first time in a church that had life. The church seated about 1200 people and hanging above the stage was a very large sign. It must have been at least 18 feet long and was painted with fireworks in all colours. In huge letters the sign said, "A Party in Freedom and Joy." "Wow," I thought. "That fits me perfectly, I like to go from one party to the next, and now I can party in the church, too." It was a fantastic feeling!

Chapter 34

A NEW CHILDHOOD

Three months after I had given my life to God, I decided to go to Bible school. The audio tapes Rick sent to me were not enough. I had only been to the church that Rick took me to five times. In Church they played fantastic music, there was even a live band on stage, and the preacher talked about God in a way I could understand. But I knew I needed to hear more on a daily basis about this God that I had received into my life. I wanted to know everything about this Jesus and I wanted to know as much as possible in the shortest possible time. I simply could not hear enough about him; I was hungry for God all the time.

Before I went on holiday I made sure to sign up for the full time Bible school at the church I attended. When I came home I started a year of life-changing teaching in the Bible school. There were about 120 students in my year and we all came from different backgrounds and denominations. I was the newest convert at the Bible school; most students had been saved for many years. Even though I had God in my life I was still struggling with my past and I was continuously thinking about the years when I was called the "whore child." I started to think if only someone had told me about

Jesus before, then I would not have needed to suffer so much and I would probably have not done so many stupid things.

Because I was struggling with my childhood memories, I started to think that other Christians could have helped me. I became very negative towards many of them, because I thought that if they had come to my night club and told me about Jesus, I would have got saved earlier. One day at Bible school, I jumped up from my chair and said to some of the other students, "Where have you been? Why didn't any of you guys come to my night club and tell me about Jesus? Why have you been keeping this a secret? You all are like 'secret agents', keeping secrets from people that they need to hear. What's the point of praying for revival when you are stuck on the seats in the churches having your own nice little time with God? Have you guys any idea that people out there don't know that there is a God and they don't know that Jesus can save them? The people out there are crying right now for a 'God' to help them out of their misery. Are you too holy to go to a disco or night club? It's not right! All you Christians know that God exists, meanwhile, I have cried for many years asking if there is a God. I am sure that I would have been saved many years ago if only some of you had just come and told me. Who is going to tell those people out there about Jesus if we don't do it? They won't find out by themselves, will they?" Many of the other students agreed with me and said we definitely needed to get serious about sharing the gospel with others.

That day I made a decision not to be like "normal" Christians, ones who kept their faith to themselves, who were too afraid to impose on other people's privacy in case they might offend them. That day I said a prayer to God and told him that I would not keep this a secret; I would tell everyone about Jesus.

Not long after I had said those words I went back to the nightclubs on my own to tell all the people there about Jesus. Obviously, this wasn't a particularly good idea, because I had just come out of that environment and that way of living. Because I was a new Christian I ended up in all sorts of situations that didn't bring me closer to God. I stumbled and fell into sin many times when I went to the night clubs. I was left devastated and filled with regret for what I had done. I was filled with condemnation for how I had hurt God and let him down after all that He had done for me.

Men had been one of my weaknesses, but I had started to want to have a husband and a man that also could be a father to my children. Sadly, the kind of man I wanted was not to be found at the night clubs. I prayed all the time that God would give me a husband that had been Christian all his life so that he could teach me everything about the Bible.

I had become very concerned when I read about King Solomon. Apparently he had 700 hundred wives and 300 concubines—a thousand women for one man alone, the equivalent of Hugh Hefner in Playboy! I was confused with that information. It was in conflict with what I had heard before, one man and one woman, but now there were a thousand women for one man. It tilted my head. I thought, "The Bible has a Hugh Hefner!" I was desperate to find a husband that knew the Bible well enough so that he could explain to me the Hugh Hefner bloke in the Old Testament who was called King Solomon.

Every evening when I had put my kids to bed I used to play my guitar and sing the new songs I had learned in Church. All the songs were about Jesus and how wonderful He was and about God's love. I was so happy and I had such a great love for God because He had accepted me as I was; I had been allowed to come to God just as I was, imperfect, with all my faults and failures. I would sing for a long time, and I felt like I was swimming in the love of God, held in his wonderful, strong arms. I felt like I was in love and that I was sitting on a pink cloud in heaven singing together with the angels.

One night when I was playing, though, I felt a heavy weight from my past pushing me down. This conflicted with the wonderful feeling I had that God was a kind and loving God and that he loved me very much. It didn't make sense that I still felt the horrible pain from the stolen years of my childhood. I was still being haunted from all the bad things that had happened to me.

In the middle of my worship to God, I put down my guitar and raised my fist to God, shaking it in anger and frustration. I shouted out to God with tears running down my cheeks, "Why, God, why? I did not ask to be born, why did you bring me into this world only to let me experience pain? Why did you create me? How could you let me go through all those bad years when I am your child? I would never have let my children go through that, I would have stopped it. Why didn't you stop it? Why, God, didn't you stop it? I was crying very hard because nothing made sense.

Suddenly out of nowhere I saw a fast film in my mind. My whole life went before me in a flash, just like those programs on TV when people speak about their near death experiences. Those people say that they had seen themselves leaving their bodies and also that they had seen their whole life played out before them, before they returned into their bodies.

I saw myself, the little girl in the cot with snow coming through the window and a frozen bottle of milk on the night table. I saw myself being rescued by Wilma from freezing to death. I saw myself in the pushchair falling into the river and almost drowning when Sally pulled me up. I saw when I was running on top of the silo and Dad was nailing planks down, and he grabbed my hand as I was falling to a sure death 30 feet below. I saw when the neighbour boy played with my Dad's rifle and aimed towards our garage to shoot, and I ran right in front of him as he pulled the trigger, only missing my head by an inch. I saw myself jumping from the barn's first floor straight through the hole where the hay was fed to the sheep. My head bounced onto the concrete flooring and I passed out, waking up in my cot hours later. I saw myself sitting outside on the stone landing where Dad had taken the rail down to be replaced by a new one. I had leaned backwards forgetting that there was no rail, and I fell down on my back eight feet below onto a flat stone.

Finally, I saw myself beaten and bruised, with a face covered with tears, walking down the road in a thick blizzard and kneeling down in the middle of the road wanting to end my life at the age of eight. I saw the bus that stopped just feet from where I was kneeling. Then I heard a loud, clear voice in my head, "WHO DO YOU THINK STOPPED THE BUS, LAILA? I was there all the time for you, my little bird; I had my hand on you all the time."

I realised then that it was God who spoke to me and that he had intervened in my life all those times. If God had not intervened, I would have been dead. I saw that He had truly looked after me, that it was impossible to have survived all those times without God rescuing me. I had moments before shaken my fist at God in anger for not being there for me, but now I raised both my arms towards Heaven and started to thank Him for saving me. I cried tears of happiness as I said sorry for thinking that He wasn't

there. I was overwhelmed with gratitude that He had been there
all the time, and that He himself had looked after me, because
there was no one else that had done that. He was the best baby
sitter anyone could ever have and I was so grateful that He had
been there all that time when I had thought I had been alone.

*****

One Saturday morning a while after I had started attending
Bible school, I was still in bed when Frank came dashing through
my bedroom door crying. He said that he wanted to move to
his dad's because he and Joel had been fighting and he said that
Joel made his life bad. Miriam followed her brothers into my
room and they all jumped into my bed. I was very tired and the
last thing I wanted in the morning was arguing kids. I started to
tell them off and tell them how lucky they were to have food on
the table and clean clothes on their bodies. I told them that they
needed to be grateful that they had a sober mum and that they
needed to be glad that their mother was alive. I had not had any of
the good things that they had, I said, and I told them how abused
I had been as a child, and how they should be ashamed to make
such a fuss over something so little.

After listening for a while, Miriam said to me, "Mum, can
you please tell us some nice stories from when you were little?
I'd like to hear that you had nice things happen to you too and
not just bad things." I realized then that I had gone over the top;
I had just gone too far. I felt very sorry for what I had done to
my kids. I so much wanted to tell Miriam a story that was nice
from my childhood, but no matter how much I tried to remember
something good, I could only remember the bad things.

How could I expect them to relate to me and therefore be happy with what they had? I realized too late that it was impossible for them to come near to comprehending what I had been through. It was not fair to them that they should know about the depth of the misery that I had lived in, expecting them to be grateful because they were treated right. I told the kids to leave my room and go and play; I simply needed to be alone.

Once the kids left me alone I cried and shouted to God, "I have no good memories from my childhood. Why God? Look what I have just done to my kids. I am a bad mother; I don't even know how to be a good mum because of what I have been through. God, both you and I know what I went through, you were there, you saw all what happened to me, you showed me a few weeks ago that you were there all the time and looked after me, but I am still messed up. I am still suffering with pain from it. God, I can't handle this at all; you have to help me."

The following week at Bible school, the Preacher was going to teach us what the Bible says about healing. He started his session by telling a story about a woman who'd had a horrible childhood, but she claimed that God had healed her and had given her a brand new childhood. As the Preacher spoke about this woman, I filled up with tears immediately. I needed a new childhood too, I was sure of that.

I could not wait for the day to be over. It was an intense subject, and it was a tough day. That night when I went to bed, I started to talk to God. "God, you were there my entire childhood and you rescued me every time. You know how much I have suffered, and you know all the pain that I am feeling on the inside. I believe that you gave that woman a new childhood, and I want to have a new childhood too.

"I know that you have no favourites, God, because I read it in the Bible the other day. It was the first line in the Bible that I marked with an orange marker. I don't know, God, if it was disrespectful of me to put a colour in the Bible, but I realized that I would have no idea where to find that word again if I didn't mark it.

"Every Saturday I give my own children candies. The three of them have the same amount of sweets, even though they are at different ages. This is because I have no favourites either. I love my kids the same. I am just a human, but you are God and you are a perfect being, and I know that when I don't want to show favouritism between my kids, you won't do it either. Therefore, God, I ask you now to also give me a new childhood just like you gave that woman. Thank you very much."

With that prayer I went to sleep. The next morning I was up early as usual, and I hurried to Bible school. As I was walking through the entrance of the Bible school a memory suddenly popped into my head. It was a lovely, hot summer's day; Angela, Ted and I were running through a field covered with beautiful flowers in all colours. The picture was like a shampoo commercial! We ran as fast as we could towards a brook near our house to have a soak in the cold water to cool us down. We chased each other through the wildflowers to see who would be the first one to jump in the brook.

I was in awe; I thought, "Wow! A good memory and also a happy one. I've never remembered that before. Have I received a new childhood? I didn't know what was happening to me, if only if only, I had a new childhood. I thought that the only way to find out if I had been given a new childhood is to find someone in the next break and tell them about some of the horrendous things that happened to me. I thought to myself that if I cried while I talked about the stories, then I didn't have a new childhood, but if I didn't cry, then I would know that I did.

And that is exactly what I did. I found a girl and told her story after story, but when I spoke I felt no pain. It was as if I spoke about something I knew about, but it had not happened to me. I knew it had happened to me, but it didn't hurt anymore. I had been bleeding all those years from the wounds from my broken childhood, but now the wounds had healed. As I talked to the girl about the wounds, it was as if I was showing her my scars where it once had hurt and bled, but new skin had now grown over it. The wounds of my past had been deep in my soul. They had bled for a long time, but not anymore. Now they were only scars, evidence of a place that once had hurt terribly, but were now healed.

As the days went by, wonderful memories unfolded like a rose. All the memories I had from the bedroom where I slept with my parents had previously been about the fighting, beatings and cigarette smoke. Now I started to remember good things from that bedroom also. I remembered that I used to jump into Mum and Dad's bed as they were sitting up in bed reading their magazines in the morning. I would bring little toy cars into the bed and play. The duvet that Mum had her legs under became my big mountain and I would let the cars run down it.

I remembered, too, that on Mother's Day or Father's Day, we used to get up really early and be very quiet so as not to wake our parents so we could bring them coffee and cake in bed. Normally Mum and Dad were early birds, but on those days they stayed in bed on purpose, pretending they were still sleeping so that we could give them coffee in bed.

I remembered when Mum baked bread, she gave me a little

lump of dough so I could make my own little loaf and she would stick it on the end of her four loaves that she had in the oven. I would wait in excitement as my bread grew and was ready like hers. I remembered, too, that before Christmas Mum would bake six or seven different kinds of biscuits and put them in large tins so that we could enjoy them during the festive season. The whole house would smell of lovely pine as Mum scrubbed the kitchen and living room from top to toe before Christmas.

I remembered, too, that before I started school, I used to be on my own with Mum. I was allowed to go with her to the barn when she was milking the cows and she allowed me to sit on the milk wagon as she drove the milk buckets down to the road for the milk lorry to pick them up. I remember helping Mum pick the eggs in the hen's house after the hens had laid them over night. One time I let Tally loose in the hen house and she chased the hens all over the place, feathers and hens flying everywhere! Mum and I laughed our heads off at that sight. And during the harvest season when we brought in the hay on the tractor, I was allowed to sit in front of the bonnet of the tractor on a seat on Mum's lap and ride the tractor into the barn with the dry hay.

All those good memories had disappeared under the dark cloud of all the bad things that had happened to me. Now they were brought back to the surface by God. I felt like a new person. I had experienced redemption and restoration in my soul. Now I could understand why God had allowed it all to happen, because He knew all the time that He was going to restore me and He knew that the pain of my childhood was going to be taken away and in such a way that it would be as if I had not had any pain at all.

When God heals, He heals. He didn't do half a job on me, He

finished His work in one night, healing me there and then in one go. I hadn't received any Christian counselling for my childhood at the church; God just gave me a brand new childhood when I asked Him for it. I didn't understand at that time that it was actually a healing that had taken place. All I knew was that I didn't have any pain when I thought or talked about those stolen years of my childhood.

*****

I also used to have a serious problem with my back. It had ached for as long as I could remember. I used to think it was because my cot had been too small and it had destroyed my back when I was a kid. At the age of 17, I had been to the doctors and they had taken x-rays to see what was wrong with my back. It turned out that my back was not as straight as it should be and that one of my legs was shorter than the other. Also all of the cushions between the discs in my spine were flat and to top it all, one of the vertebrae was missing in my lower spine. The doctors said that unfortunately there was nothing they could do to help with my back and the pain that was caused from no space between the discs. I could put an insole in one of my shoes to help with the different length of my legs, but the pain would still be there. The doctors said I would have to learn to live with the pain for the rest of my life.

One day at Bible school during the prayer hour, I had excruciating pain in my back; I was unable to stand for a long time. I sat down many times and stood up again. One of the students asked me why I was sitting down as we were supposed to stand. I told him that I had to continually change position as my back hurt so much. He said I should have told him earlier so that he could have prayed for me. I didn't believe, I told him, that people were healed when others laid hands on them. God didn't have the time to heal people's backs; he would probably be too busy trying to keep those poor starving children in Africa alive. At the same time, in my mind I also thought, "I wish that God was so good that he could heal my back."

My eyes were closed and suddenly that man laid his hands on my back and I felt a warm tingling feeling. The pain went away! Tears were running down my cheeks as I thought that God is indeed so good that he healed my back. I was over the moon with excitement; I could not wait to find a sick person that I could pray for, because this worked, God heals people through us.

I ran around the Bible school asking if anyone was sick so I could pray for them. I expected God to heal them, because I knew he had no favourites. Even when I picked up Miriam and Joel at Kindergarten I stopped people and asked if they were sick so that I could pray for them. Sometimes I didn't even ask if I could pray for people; if the situation didn't allow me to ask, then I just made sure to lay my hands on them anyway to try to smuggle in a healing whilst I was praying on the inside for God to heal them. I would slap them on their shoulders saying "Good to see you" while I was actually praying for their healing. Everywhere I went, I was looking for people that were sick. I loved it that God was so good that He healed people that were suffering in pain. I also loved that God wanted to use my hands to heal.

Chapter 35

THE YEAR OF MIRACLES

I loved it at Bible school and 1993 and 1994 went by very quickly. I was plugged into the Church, and I loved going every Sunday to hear what was preached. But storm clouds were beginning to form.

I started to understand that Jim had doubts that he was Joel's biological father. I knew I was sitting on a time bomb and needed to do something. I went to a counsellor at my Church and explained the situation. I told the whole story of how I had become pregnant and that I had kept this a secret for five years. The reason I had not said anything was that I had wanted to protect Joel. I told the counsellor that I felt that I had lived a lie and I didn't want to lie any more, now that I had become a Christian. I wasn't sure who was the father of my son, even though my gut feeling told me it was the man I had met on holiday. The counsellor advised me to tell the truth if I was ever asked, and I agreed that it would be the best thing to do.

Just a few weeks later, Jim confronted me and asked me if he was Joel's dad. I told him that there was another man involved at that time but I wasn't sure; it could be either of them. Jim demanded that I organize a DNA test to see who Joel's father was. I organised a test and it was clear that the other man was Joel's dad.

I was in a big dilemma. How on earth was I going to break this devastating news to my kids? How would a five year old kid react to the news that his dad was not his dad? I decided to tell the two oldest kids first. We jumped up onto Miriam's bed and I said to them that I had something important to tell them. I told them what I had done all those years ago because I had been so lonely all the time back then and that I had fallen for this man because he flirted with me a lot. Miriam looked at me with round tearful eyes and said, "Mum, does that mean that Joel is only our half brother?"

"Yes, he is your half brother," I said. "Joel would not be Joel, if the other man wasn't his father, so in that way it is good."

Then Miriam said, "Since Joel is only our half brother, that means that we have to take extra good care of him and look after him even more. We really need to be nice to him, don't we?"

"Yes," I told her. "That is a good way of looking at it. Let us all be extra kind to Joel."

Once I had chatted with the two oldest I asked Joel to come into the room. I explained in the best way I could to a five year old kid that the man he knew as his dad, Jim, was not his father. I told him that Jim would always be like a dad for him, and that he had another one too. Joel's eyes filled up with tears and he said, "Oh, I have two dads. Then where is my other dad?"

"Yes," I said "You have two dads." Then I told the kids the very little I knew about Joel's biological dad. I decided from then on only to bring the subject up if the kids asked me any more questions in the future.

*****

I experienced many miracles in 1994 and 1995.

I had very little money and I was totally drained in my body, I was always tired and I suffered a lot with being dizzy. I could not afford to buy any supplements or any fruit or orange juices to help my immune system. I remember going shopping with a tiny shopping list, getting only the most necessary items of food. I walked around the shop with my shopping trolley with a lump in my throat. I saw all the other customers filling up their trolleys until the food was overflowing. I had very few items in my trolley and I needed so much more.

This time I could not even afford to buy flour to bake bread; I simply didn't have enough money. I hoped the bread I had baked which I had left in the freezer would last me a few more days. I passed on the cucumbers, they were simply too expensive at £1. Miriam loved cucumber, and I so much wanted to buy one for her. I had to pass on the peppers, too. I loved them, and they would be lovely to put in a casserole, but at £1.50 for one, there was no way I could afford them. I passed the milk counter to pick up some milk, and next to the milk were the yogurts, and I noticed that they came in 1 litre cartons. Stacked next to them was the chocolate and strawberry milk my kids loved. I wished I could pick up just a litre of yogurt and take it home to surprise my kids and give them a treat.

I added up the cost of the food in my trolley on the calculator that I had, and saw that there was no way at all that I could buy anything extra. It was very hard to hold back my tears as I left the shop. I simply could not buy anything extra for my kids. One small bag of Harribos was all I could afford to give them for their Saturday candy, and the bag was shared between them.

The very next day my doorbell rang. Outside stood an older woman I had met at Church. She had visited me before as I had once invited her for coffee after Church. She said she had been to the shop and she had loads of stuff in her car if I was interested in receiving some food. She said, "This food is the stuff the shop is throwing out, because it has passed its sell by date, but there is nothing wrong with any of it, just bits here and there. Some of it you can just cut off where it is starting to go bad."

She carried bag after bag into my kitchen. The first bag was filled with 1 litre containers of different flavours of yogurt! Also in that bag were several litres of chocolate and strawberry milk. The expiry date was over by two days but I tasted one of the yoghurts and it was fine. The next bag she brought in was filled with cucumbers; I went through all the cucumbers and cut off the bad parts. The next bag was full of peppers—red, yellow, and green. Then a whole big bag of oranges. The last bag she brought in contained loaves of breads of all sorts, and also in the bag were lovely Danish pastries. My heart felt like it was about to jump out of my chest in excitement. These were the very items I had to pass up in the shop the day before. I threw my arms up in the air and shouted, "Thank you Jesus! Thank you God! You provide for me, and I love you so much."

For one year I had provision from that lady receiving all sorts of food from the shop. The lady had spoken to the shop manager and he made sure that the food was stored in a way that it could be eaten. I ended up having so much food that I was able to share with other people too. I was happy to cut off the rotten parts of the fruit and vegetables. I was not fussy, I washed and cleaned it all. With the apples and pears I made desserts, the peppers I chopped and cleaned and put in my freezer to use in casseroles. The carrots, cauliflowers and broccoli I would boil slightly, and then mix them together and freeze them for later use. With the soft oranges I made orange juice and drank lovely fresh orange juice every day, and I got my strength back, with all that Vitamin C.

Just like the prophet Elijah who had received food through a raven, I received food through that woman. I was so grateful to God that he provided for me through her. I literally lived off the food from the shop's rubbish bin for a year.

*****

Frank and Miriam walked to school every day. It was about a two mile walk down a steep hill to their school. A bus was put on for the children, but you had to pay to be on it. I had no money for a bus pass, so my kids would walk to and from school every day on their own, with the bus passing them on the way with all the children on it. Miriam started to say she wished for a pink bike that had gears. I told her that there was no way I could afford to buy her a bike. I felt very sorry for Frank and Miriam as they had to walk to school. Miriam said that she would pray to Jesus so that He could give her a pink bike. I said, go on, just pray, God is good.

A few weeks later I was visiting my friend that lived on the same estate. She always passed on the clothes from her kids to me and she was a very good friend. As we were chatting about what we had been doing the last week, she said to me that she had been tidying up in her garage and she had so much rubbish to chuck out. "By the way," she said, "I have two bikes you can have if you are interested. They are in really good condition and it would be such a shame to chuck them on the rubbish tip." When I went out behind the garage to pick up the bikes I saw a pink girl's bike with three gears. Again I cried in gratitude that God had answered my daughter's prayer for a pink bike.

Chapter 36

SILLY AND IMPATIENT DECISIONS

Since I first got saved, I had prayed that God would give me a husband. I had no problem being single when I went to Bible school. But after a while I started to long for a husband and a father for my kids. I was not used to being single, and I was getting more and more impatient about finding a husband. I felt I had become a mature Christian and that I was ready to marry. I was 29 years of age, I had been saved for two years, been to Bible school and I didn't want to be alone anymore. I also wanted to get married before I turned thirty.

I had gotten to know a few people when I went to Bible school, but I had not yet met anyone that I would fall in love with. After a while I started to go to the cinema and hang out with a guy from my church. I wasn't particularly interested in him at first; I just loved to hang out with a member of the opposite sex for a change. This man kept visiting me all the time and I liked the company also. I did fall in love with him after a few weeks and we started to date. I was so silly and impatient that I literally threw myself onto this man. For such a long time I had longed for physical contact, like hugging and holding a man, not to mention kissing and also sex. That had been my life before I was saved, and I was pulled in that direction when I started to date him. I had been single for two years, and sadly I was not strong enough to resist sleeping with this man. Afterwards, I was totally gutted and ashamed because, of course, again, I had let God, my loving father, down. I wanted to make things right between my Heavenly father and myself, so when this man proposed and asked me to marry him, I said yes.

We dated only five months when we got married, and even though I had many warnings in my guts not to marry, I still went ahead. Even my church said they didn't want to marry us until we had dated one year. But I was stubborn and didn't listen. I knew I had sinned and I thought I would make things right by getting married.

We married at the end of 1995. Once married, I cried every evening for the first year because of our financial situation. I had started to work to get more money, but the financial situation went down the drain. All our arguments concerned finances. I felt he didn't bring in any money. I eventually had to empty all my kids' bank accounts, all the money they had received when they were christened, which totalled several thousand pounds, and I sold my car to pay off my new husband's various credit cards and loans. I hoped that by doing this our financial situation would get better, but unfortunately nothing changed by my sacrifice. There was still not enough money to live on, and things went from bad to worse.

In the new year of 1999, after three years of marriage, we had a massive argument over the financial situation. We went to bed and the next day my husband went to work before me. When I arrived at work I sent him an email to say we had to find a solution to our financial problems, it simply could not continue the way it was. A few minutes after I sent the email to him, I received a reply saying that he had left me and I must not try to find him or contact him. He had picked up his clothes and he was out.

I was devastated. I simply could not believe what I was reading, I tried to call him but he didn't answer his phone. I was unable to continue my work and my boss said it was okay for me to go home. There was no way I felt I could go home, I needed to try to get help. I went straight from work to my church for counselling, almost unable to see where I was driving because of my tears.

It didn't make sense; all couples argue now and again, but they don't leave because of a silly argument. I had been in many relationships before I became a Christian, but I had never experienced in my entire life a man just walking out like that. He filed for separation a few weeks later and one year later we were divorced. Once he picked up the rest of his stuff, I never saw him again.

During this time I was unable to get proper sleep and when I went to bed I would write letters to him in my mind, asking him, "How could you, how could you, after all I have done for you?" I lost my appetite and lots of weight very quickly. I felt like a total failure. I had prayed so much to find a Christian husband and I had failed again. I failed as a non-Christian and I also failed as a Christian. I thought I had heard from God that this was the man I was going to marry. I had not liked him at first but I had prayed to God and said, "If I start to like him, he is for me." Silly me. I didn't listen to the other warnings prior to marrying this man. I should have at least listened when my Church would only agree to marry us after we had dated for a year. If I had waited one year I might never have married him.

After many weeks of counselling, my counsellors said to me that I had to forgive him. Jesus had forgiven us our sins and we had to forgive one another. I had a massive problem forgiving him for leaving me. I told them I didn't want to be a hypocrite, that I was unable to forgive him because I was still angry with him. My feelings told me that I wanted to find him and tie him to a chair and tape his mouth shut, and then I would tell him what I thought of him. After that I would spit deep green spit from the back of my throat straight into his face, followed by scratching his face with my nails till he bled; then I would finish him off by kicking his ankles so hard they would break and he would not be able to walk.

My counsellors said forgiveness is not a feeling, it's a choice. They said the same way you chose to receive Jesus into your life, you choose to forgive. "Forgiveness doesn't make him right, it sets you free." I said that I wanted to forgive him but because of all the feelings I had I'd rather hurt him than forgive him. The counsellors said, "It's just a choice you have to make, and it is as simple as that." I said I would like to do that, and right there I spoke out loudly with my counsellors as witnesses that I forgave him for leaving me.

I also asked my counsellors if God could take the feelings and the love I had for this man away. They said, "If you have faith to do so, you can ask God to remove them." And so I did, and the most amazing thing happened. The following day I picked up some photos from the previous Christmas and I looked at the pictures of the man I had been married to for three years. I was absolutely amazed that I had really been married to him. I suddenly saw him with different eyes, and I was unable to understand how on earth I could have found him attractive at all. Looking at the photos I found him rather ugly, and I shuddered with the thought that he had even touched me. All the feelings and the love I had for that man was totally gone. It was a true miracle; it is impossible to explain how it happened and how my feelings could leave so quickly after that prayer.

Even though all the feelings I had for this man went just like that, and I had accepted what he had done, I still struggled to accept what I had done and to understand and accept why I had been so stupid as to marry him. "How could I have been so silly? Why didn't I see that I never should have married him and why didn't I pay attention to the red lights that I'd had in my guts during the time we dated? What's wrong with me? I thought I had heard from God, and now I knew that I didn't."

I became very depressed and frustrated. I had been saved for five years, and I didn't even know how to find a proper husband. I even had thoughts that maybe the Christian life was not for me, and I felt that it would be very embarrassing to go to church being such a failure. But I hated the thought of not going to church either; I simply didn't know what to do.

One warm spring evening I sat outside in my garden and shared a beer with my neighbour. I was very disillusioned and we shared one beer after another. By three o'clock in the morning and I don't know how many beers later, we said, "Up yours" to everything and everyone, and we had sorted the whole world out. I was very tired and in the end I staggered off to bed to get some sleep. The alarm clock buzzed just four hours later, and I was in no fit state to get up and drive to work, I was still not sober. I had a massive hangover from the night before. I skived my job that day and I didn't even care. It had gone from bad to worse; getting drunk certainly didn't solve any problems. I didn't repeat that event again and I always went to work from then on.

One afternoon I rang one of my mentors in the Church and I cried and moaned saying how hard I found it, and how my life was ruined. I told her that I wanted to give up. I said I felt like I was standing on the edge of a cliff and I wanted to throw myself off and just die, and I wanted God to catch me and take me to Heaven. The thought of suicide was sometimes a thought that rose up in the back of my mind at times when I had gone through bad things.

I was expecting a bit of sympathy for my bad situation, but instead, this woman who I'd never heard say "Boo to a goose" before, raised her voice in a passionate but not angry way, and said, "Laila, don't you dare tempt the Lord your God, The Almighty. Your life is not over because of a man or a marriage that has ended. Look at everything you have been through and survived up to now. You are not a quitter because of a man. Do you mean to tell me that you are going to allow a man to make you like some of the angry and bitter women I see and hear about? In their fifties and sixties, they are still bitter and angry and complaining about things that happened to them years ago and they blame the men that hurt them for the situation that they are in now. You have your whole life ahead of you, and you had better get on with it right now." It was the exact "slap" I needed, it literally woke me up.

As she was speaking I saw myself ending up just like those women I had also heard of and seen, if I continued down the road of self pity. Suddenly it felt like a giant was rising up on the inside. I had been beaten and I felt I had been down for the count, but now that slap woke me up and I was able to get up onto my feet and fight again. I saw how stupid I was to even have been thinking of giving up. That was not me at all. I had always managed to get back up. I was determined that I was going to make it, and that I was not going to allow this marriage breakdown to destroy me. I had survived my whole childhood and I was definitely not going to allow this "jerk" or any other "jerks" to turn me into an angry, bitter old woman, just as I had seen my own Nan become.

I became determined to move on with my life again and the first step I took was to try to understand how I could have missed hearing from God concerning marrying this man. The most important thing for me was that I needed to know that God was speaking to me and that I would recognise His voice. I was terrified by the thought of not hearing from God.

The following week I went to Church again, having decided that I needed to hear a word from God. I went with the hope that when the preacher was preaching he would say something that would be relevant to my situation and I would be able to make sense of how I could have been so stupid. There was nothing in the sermon concerning my situation, however, and after the meeting was finished I went into the Church canteen and sat down at a table with my kids. I thought, "I have to have an answer; maybe God will send someone to my table to speak to me." The kids were nagging to go home, and they were hungry; I could not afford to buy them any waffles, but I told them firmly that I had to sit there for a while. I needed to get a word from someone.

First I chatted with a family for a while, and when they left I felt sad that they had not given me a word from God. The kids nagged me all the time to go home but I told them that they had to wait for just a few minutes more. I didn't want to give up; I waited and waited. Then one of the guys I had used to hang with a bit when I first got saved sat down at my table and asked me how I was doing. He had been to Russia and evangelised the people there.

I said, "How are things? Do you want the honest truth? 'Crap,' that is how things are. I went from one hell to another when I was unsaved, then I got saved and nothing changed. I have gone from one hell to another."

He said, "You will always find the answers in the Bible."

That got me a bit provoked, because there was still so many things I didn't understand in the Bible.

I told him, "The Bible is a very thick book with hundreds of hundreds of pages; you can't just find your answer suddenly in there amongst all those pages. My problem is just too complicated."

"Look at Jesus," he said.

"Jesus is the son of God," I said. "He is divine."

"Jesus is also a man and he prayed all night before he chose his 12 disciples, and among the twelve he also chose Judas. But when you look at the story you will see that it was Judas that chose to betray Jesus."

The penny dropped, it all made sense. Yes, Jesus was the son of God, and he had also prayed the whole night before he chose all 12 disciples, but it was Judas' choice to betray Jesus. That was not Jesus' choice. Suddenly I didn't feel so bad that I had chosen to marry that man after praying about it. The man I married chose to leave me, it wasn't my choice for him to leave, it was his choice alone.

Chapter 37

THE POWER OF FORGIVENESS

A few weeks later, in May of 1999, Frank was going to have his graduation from the Teenage Bible School he had been attending for a year. I invited close family to be a part of his big day. In the Norwegian culture the Lutheran churches have their confirmation ceremonies, but we were not a part of that church, and our church had their own graduation service for their students. All the grandparents were invited and also my dad. I was very surprised that Dad drove the long journey from the west to attend Frank's big day.

I didn't understand until later why Dad came to the graduation, and I do think it had to do with the conversation I had with Dad seven months earlier. Then I had received a phone call from Dad who was complaining about a family argument that had taken place and he wanted me to try to make peace in the family. I told Dad I was not interested in being the third part of this disagreement as this was a deal between him and the other person.

Then suddenly out of nowhere, without even thinking about it, I confronted him about what he had done to me during my childhood. I told him that I had only asked him to help me one time in my whole life. I had asked him about a year earlier to borrow some money to buy a car and I was going to pay him back in three months time, when I had my tax return. Dad had inherited a lot of money from his auntie and I knew he could afford it.

I told Dad that I felt he "cut" one hand off me when I was a child the way he rejected me out of all his children and how his words and beatings had ruined my childhood. He had "cut" off my other hand, I told him, when I had asked him to borrow money I so desperately needed. But after that I said to him, "I want you to know, Dad, that you can die and go to your grave knowing that I have forgiven you for what you have done to me. You ruined my childhood, and I was in such a mess because of what you did that I also had to seek help from a psychiatrist. You stole all those years from me, but I want you to know I have forgiven you."

I told him about a conversation that I had had with Ted several years earlier, in which, he suddenly told me that he regretted how he had treated me many years ago. I continued to say to Dad, "You have never ever said sorry, but still I want you to always remember, Dad, that I have forgiven you; I hold no grudges about what you did."

I could hardly believe what came out of my own mouth; I don't know why I confronted him at that time. It was also strange that though I knew I had forgiven Dad, I was angry with him when I was confronting him with what he had done. The closest way I can describe how I felt when I spoke to him on the phone was as if a big dam had burst and the water gushed out from where it had been held back. I wanted him to know that he had hurt me, but at the same time I didn't want him to hurt.

Dad said it wasn't easy for him when he was a kid either; he had asked his dad to borrow £3 for petrol when Angela was born so he could visit Mum at the hospital, and his dad didn't give it to him. And by the way he said, "It wasn't until 1976 that things got bad." 1976, that year went through my head. "He knows, he knows, because that was the year when Mum left him but later returned. It was then most of the hell broke loose in my life and lasted until I left home in 1982." My life had also been very bad before 1976, before Mum had left Dad, but when she came home, Dad seemed to turn all his anger towards me as if he wanted someone to blame. From then on Dad didn't dare to hit Mum anymore in case she would leave him again and I became the target of all his anger.

I told Dad that I had never abused my kids just because I had experienced abuse myself. I had never rejected them, because I had been rejected, and I had never beaten them because I had been beaten. I wanted Dad to own up, and I told him his excuse was pathetic, but I strongly emphasised that he didn't need to worry, because I held no grudges and I had forgiven him.

Once the conversation was over and I put the phone down, I sobbed and sobbed. I had confronted my Dad; I had never known if Dad really knew what he had done to me. I knew I had forgiven him many years ago, though I don't know where or when. It was not like I had made a decision to forgive him like I had done with my husband that had left me. With Dad I had just forgiven him, not consciously knowing when I had done it. In the bottom of my heart I knew it was important to tell him that I had forgiven him. It was so strange because I had never planned to call him and bring it up; it just seemed to flow out from me when Dad called and wanted to talk about something totally different.

So now seven months after this conversation with Dad on the

phone, the graduation for Frank was due. Dad came to celebrate his grandson's graduation from teenage Bible school. I had prepared a lovely elk roast for dinner and 15 guests attended. There were several speeches at the dinner table, first Jim's parents, then Jim gave a speech, and then Dad got up from his chair. I didn't know what to do, because I knew Dad never gave speeches. Dad started his speech, "This is Frank's special day, and I wish him the best, but it has probably not been very easy for Frank being the oldest and all."

Then Dad's speech changed from being about Frank to being about me. I almost fell off my chair as Dad spoke. It was very moving. I don't know how I managed not to cry.

"I know that it certainly hasn't been easy for Laila," he said. "It must have been very difficult for her to grow up in our home, but I am really proud of how she has turned out, being a very good mother for her children despite of all the things she has been through. As parents we make loads of mistakes and I have made loads of mistakes concerning how I brought up my children, but I am so glad that I can see how Laila has turned out, despite what she has been through."

I can't remember everything Dad said after that because I was so overwhelmed by emotion.

I knew this was Dad's way of saying sorry. It was a wonderful feeling and I knew this was something he knew he had to do. I do believe that when I had confronted him seven months earlier with what he did to me, and told him that I had forgiven him, I believe that set him free from all the guilt he must have carried for many years. I believe that after Mum's death, Dad had had all the rubbish kicked out of him, he had become more humble. I could see that he had become a different man.

Dad could not say sorry to Mum as she was dead, but maybe this was his way of saying sorry to those he had hurt who were still alive. I knew in my heart that Dad must have regretted all that he had done and I believe that he probably wished he could have gone back in time and done it all differently if he had the chance.

After that day, I never felt strange in Dad's presence. I always used to be on edge when I was near Dad, but after that day I had no problem sitting and just having an ordinary conversation with him. A couple of months went by and I felt completely restored in all the areas of my life. I didn't carry any guilt because my husband had left me, I was happy and content to be alone, and I wasn't afraid to be a single mum anymore. And the greatest part was that I had started having a relationship with Dad.

Chapter 38

DISCOVERING MY DESTINY

The Church annual summer conference was due. It was July of 1999. I always loved the conferences that the Church put on. There were always preachers from around the world and it was great to hear what God was doing in other parts of the world. I had painted my wooden house the previous year, but I had not had time to finish painting inside my garage. The weather was lovely, and I decided to spend Sunday painting my garage so that I could enjoy the conference for the rest of the week.

I was on the ladder inside my garage, almost finished painting, when suddenly I felt the urge to start to pray. I prayed for a few minutes, then as I was trying to reach a difficult area in the garage with my paintbrush, the ladder collapsed and I fell down six feet and landed on my coccyx. I was unable to move, the pain was so excruciating. I shouted for help and one of my neighbours came over to help me. I was in such pain that I could not get up on my feet, and the neighbour called for my sister to take me to the hospital. Thankfully nothing was broken and after a few hours I was able to leave the hospital. I stayed at my sister's house that night on a mattress in her lounge downstairs; I was unable to walk up the stairs to the bedroom.

I was totally gutted; I had really looked forward to the summer conference and now I could not even walk without excruciating pain. I had to crawl across the floor to get anywhere. The following night I stayed home and my kids had to fetch my mattress from my bed so I could sleep on the floor in my lounge. Now I had missed two days of the conference and I didn't know what to do. I had looked forward to this conference for a whole year. It was a great highlight in the church calendar. I became determined to go, even if I had to crawl into my car and into church and lie on the floor and listen to the preachers.

Thankfully I was a little bit better on the third day and I decided to go to Church no matter what. I limped to my car and drove down to the church. I had taken a pillow to use when I sat on a chair, I was unable to sit straight up and I was almost lying down on the chair and falling off the edge of the seat to avoid sitting on my coccyx.

There was a preacher from Africa that evening. I didn't care about the pain I had in my back, I was just so happy to be at the conference. At the end of the service, the preacher said that he always used to pray and pray before he was going to preach. He would ask God to be with him, and the Holy Spirit and Jesus to help him. One day he said he was praying to God like that, pleading with God about this request before he ministered to the people. Then God suddenly spoke to him and said, "Why do you pray that I shall be with you and then the Holy Spirit be with you and then for Jesus to be with you? Why do you pray like that? You have received Jesus as Lord in your life and now you have the whole kingdom of God living inside you. When you go to minister to people. you take Jesus with you because he lives inside you."

I thought that was brilliant. Wow! The whole Trinity is living inside me! That means that even if I fell down from the moon and broke all the bones in my body, Jesus lives inside me and I can do all things through him. It was fantastic to think of it like that. Jesus took all the pain on Calvary, and by his stripes we are healed, no matter what has happened to us. With that revelation I got up from my chair and I leant forward to touch the floor with my hands. All the pain I had in my back from falling off the ladder and landing on my coccyx went there and then. I was healed in one moment, not one hint of discomfort was left where the pain had been. I was so happy that I jumped up and down and shouted "yippee!"

But I was due for another treat.

There were five more days left of the conference and I was so happy that God had healed me once more, and I was going to be attending the meeting without pain. The following day was a highlight for me; a funny man from Wales was going to preach at the church. I had heard him many times before, and I always found him hilarious. His name was Ray Bevan. He was the only preacher my kids wanted to listen to; he managed to get the attention of every age group in the Church.

Ray preached a very good message and at the end of his sermon he started to share some personal trauma that he had gone through. He had experienced divorce which he said was the worst thing that he had gone through in his whole life. He didn't say anything about who left who; he didn't talk badly about his ex-wife in any way. He just spoke openly about how hard he had found it as a preacher to go through such a horrible thing.

As Ray was preaching about the misery he had been through, I was very encouraged. I thought, "A preacher going through divorce, so it doesn't just happen to ordinary people like me then?" I had thought that it must be so much easier for preachers; they know God much more than I do. I felt so encouraged to hear that preachers can fail too. I had never heard any preacher share about their failures before. I thought, "There must be hope for me then, when even a great preacher can't make it, maybe it wasn't so strange that I couldn't make it either."

After the sermon Joel wanted to get Ray's autograph. I told my 10 year old that he had to hurry because the preachers always shot out from the main hall to the green room straight after the service. Joel didn't obey me like he always did; he waited and waited and I said to him it would be too late if he didn't hurry. Suddenly Joel shot off like a bullet and there my little son stood talking to Ray. Joel had just started to learn English in school, and he didn't know a lot. Then both Joel and Ray approached me and Ray asked me if I was related to this little boy. I said that I was his Mum.

Then I said to Ray, "Thank you so much for being so honest and sharing that you have been through a divorce. I am going through a similar thing myself now, and I was so encouraged to hear that you have been through the same." Ray said it was the first time he shared publicly that he was divorced and that he felt that it would help people to get back on their feet. The chat I had with Ray was no longer than that. Then he said to me very pastorally, as he shook my hand to go, "God bless you. God has someone really special for you." And then he walked off to the green room.

As Ray shook my hand and said God has someone really special for you, a LOUD voice spoke to me in my head and I knew it was God. He said, "IT IS HIM". I could not believe my own thoughts—no way. "It is him!"

But I don't want to have a man! I am not ready for anything at the moment. I'd prefer to hate men for at least two years before I even think of getting involved with anyone. I went home and hardly slept that night. I got up in the middle of the night praying and trying to convince God that he was wrong. In the end I gave up, and I said to God, "Okay, Your way then. If I am the woman this man needs, I will make myself available to him, but You, God, must arrange for us to meet. I am not running after anyone."

The following evening service Ray was preaching again and I was just hanging out in the foyer at the Church. There were hundreds of people around. Suddenly I bumped into Ray there. We just had a small chat, and I asked him where his Church was. I told him about a woman I had met on holiday from England whom I had led to the Lord and I wanted to find a good church for her. I thought that this was great. I can tell that British woman I had got to know on holiday about Ray's church and send her there. Then other people wanted the attention of the preacher and I went into the canteen to see if I could find some friends to chat with. I eventually went home and hardly slept again the second night.

The following day Ray was preaching again. After the service I had just bought a cup of coffee and a waffle and was about to sit down at a table in the canteen. Then I saw Ray poke his head through the door. I don't know how I knew, but I knew that he was going into the canteen to look for me. I put my tray down on the table, and I walked as fast as I could without running to catch up with him before he went downstairs into the greenroom. Ray was so fast that I missed him by about six feet before the door slammed right in front of me and he was gone.

I thought, how stupid of me to think he wanted to see me; maybe I was wrong about what I had heard that day. But I did feel that we were supposed to meet. I went home the third night and I hardly slept that night either. The following day was Ray's last sermon, and as he finished another preacher was going to preach straight away. I had decided to go up to Ray and give him my address after the service before he went home. There was no way I was going to contact him. He was the man, and I was really not fussed in the first place, I didn't fancy him at all.

But I felt almost compelled to act. I felt that God had spoken to me and that I had to be obedient to the Lord. I didn't know how on earth I was going to manage to give him the little piece of paper with my address. I didn't dare walk forward to where all the preachers were standing and talking. I waited and waited, and then suddenly Ray walked towards the door. I panicked; I knew that this was definitely not supposed to happen. I got up from my chair and walked rapidly out of the exit on the opposite side of the stage. I caught up with Ray in the foyer where some people had already stopped to talk to him. I walked firmly up to Ray and said, "Excuse me, can I talk with you for a minute?"

Ray said, "Yes of course, just wait one second. I will be right with you."

About two seconds later Ray was standing in front of me and said, "How can I help you?"

I don't know why I said what I said; it was the strangest way to open a conversation. I said, "I have not slept for almost three nights. I don't know what is going on here, but I think you know what I mean."

Ray looked at me seriously and said, "Yes, I do know what you mean."

We chatted for a while and I gave him the piece of paper with my address and he left to go back home. There was absolutely no flirting between us at all; it was all serious and it had God's fingerprint all over it.

Ray informed my pastor that he had met me. He also asked him about the situation concerning the husband who had left me. Ray asked my pastor if he had his blessing to get to know me. My pastors knew everything about my situation because I had received counselling from the church when my husband had left.

During the following nine months from July of 1999 to April 2000, Ray and I spent about 400 hours on the phone just talking and getting to know each other as friends. My divorce came through in April of 2000. We eventually fell in love with each other and Ray proposed when I went to visit Wales at Easter in 2000. Our legal documents to marry were arranged in Norway at my Church, because I wanted my own pastor to marry us, and he wasn't licensed to marry abroad. We put the date as near as we could to the wedding party that was going to be held in Wales. We had spoken for four hundred hours on the phone and seen each other only fifteen days before we got married.

In June of 2000 I sold my house and my car. I left all my family and friends and everything that was familiar to me and moved to Wales with my three children. I left my culture and my country for good. I felt like Peter, when Jesus asked him to come and walk on the water; the only difference between me and Peter was that Peter had a boat to go back to, but I had burned the boat; there was nothing for me to go back to. Our wedding ceremony was led by my pastor from Norway and the party was celebrated on July 22nd of 2000 at King's Church in Newport and we count that as our wedding day.

Epilogue

Four years after our wedding, I received a telephone call from Dad. He said that he wanted to give me a tiny farm that he had inherited from one of his uncles. He asked if I would be interested in having it; he would give it to me for nothing. I was over the moon with happiness that Dad wanted to give me this little farm. This was the house my Granny had grown up in and her mother, my Great Grandmother, had been a full on Christian. This was the house that used to be so dirty, and I would go together with Granny to help her scrub the kitchen and the living room from top to toe. (It was also the same house that I had stolen money from 24 years earlier, for which, sadly, as a child, I had no remorse.) I had many happy memories, though, from this house, because all those who lived there had been so happy. Even though the house was very dirty, it was not the dirt that was stuck in my memory—it was the laughter and fun that always filled it, not to mention all the cakes, sweets, and pop, I was always allowed to eat as much of as I wanted!

Ray and I went over to this beautiful place in the west of Norway to take a look at the state of the farm. The house was fine. It was solid and the roof was only 15 years old, but it needed a proper facelift and a few coats of paint. The property had a barn, a garage and an outhouse too, and in the outhouse was the WC and bathroom. But we needed to make a bathroom and toilet inside. We spent one month each summer for the next five years doing up the house and now it looks great. We even have our own waterfall that runs by the back of the house, where Ray fishes for trout every day to his great pleasure. Two years after we had the house, the farmers in the area also built a mini power station that gives us income from the electric power that is sold. This income covers all the expenses that we have on this farm.

It is so wonderful, I had left everything that was familiar to me when I moved to Wales, but God has given me back far more than I can ever think or comprehend.

Ray and I have been happily married for over ten years as I finished the final work on this book in September of 2010. My children are adults now, and I have also become a grandmother to the most beautiful little girl in the world. My calling is first of all to be a wife to Ray and to spread the good news about the kingdom of God. Ray preaches all around the world and I also travel with him and speak at many churches too.

I head up the Women's Ministry at our church called "Free to Fly." I often speak about the pain and trauma I went through during my childhood, not to have a pity party, but to give hope to people that even though we go through a lot of pain, God heals, restores and delivers.

I am a living example that God is a good God, and that He performs miracles by restoring and healing broken people. I hope that I have managed to show in my book what God can do with a broken and hurt little girl, raising her up and using her as a tool for His Kingdom, to bring restoration, and healing, and hope.

Last but not least. The Lord Jesus Christ completely forgives us for our sins and when he wipes them away he remembers them no more.

If he can do this for me, he can do it for you.

A Personal Letter to the Reader

Dear Reader,

I want to take this opportunity to thank you for the journey you have taken by reading my book. Like any tunnel, there is light at the end of it. For 27 years I felt that I was trapped inside a long, dark tunnel, and I had been stuck there for so long I could not find my way out. I didn't escape from the tunnel until I got to know the Lord Jesus Christ. When I prayed on the phone with my cousin one spring evening in 1993, I began the journey to break the camp I had set up for myself inside the tunnel. Though my walk with Jesus was full of stumbling in the beginning, I kept on walking with Him, no matter what happened. I became so in love with my wonderful saviour that I walked with Him step by step in the direction He showed me, to find that one day I was out of the darkness.

Romans 2:11 says, *"For God shows no partiality or undue favour or unfairness; with Him one man is not different from another."* (Amplified Bible)

This was the first sentence I underlined in the Bible, and it was the first revelation I had. It was a word from God for me. This word is also for you: God has no favourites.

You have read my story and maybe you can identify with me because you also have gone through your hell. I have taken you with me on my journey, where I have shared the most personal experiences in my life, for a reason. Because I know that God wants to do for you what he did for me. The only reason I decided to write this book was for you. I wrote it to give you a hope and a future.

Do you remember when I wrote in the book about asking God to give me a new childhood? I had heard the preacher talk in Bible school about a woman who had claimed she had been given a new childhood. I knew that I qualified to have a new childhood too, because of the hell I had been through. I thought to myself, I am only a human being and I consider myself to be fair. I love all my children just the same and I don't give one of them more than the other. How much more does God, the very creator of the whole universe and everything that exists, and so full of Love for His creation, want to give me also a new childhood. That is what I pray this book will do for you. I pray you will realize how very deeply God loves you and that what He did for me, He wants to do for you.

I used to love to go to conferences at my local church in Norway. I would sit in the pews as near to the front as I could so that I could see everyone that was ministering. I thoroughly enjoyed all the preaching and the seminars that were held. I used to pay special attention to the preachers' wives. I would admire them as they elegantly entered the auditorium to sit down at the front. I thought what a wonderful life they must have, wearing lovely clothes and makeup and jewellery. These women in the ministry are really doing something of purpose in their lives, I thought, they must be the happiest women on earth. I thought it must be so easy for these women, living lives like that; they would not even know what pain and trauma is. I believed that you had to be perfect to do the work of God, and that with a background like mine there was never any hope that I could make a difference in someone's life.

There was one particular woman from South Africa that used to come with her husband that I liked the best of all of them. She was so beautiful with her black hair and her pale skin which made her face shine; to me she looked like a movie star from Hollywood. Just looking at her made me content. I thought this woman was untouched by pain; she seemed so pure that God must have kept her in his arms all the time.

One day this lady got up to the platform to speak. It's impossible for me to describe all the details of this story, it's a book in itself, but I will just tell some of it.

She began by talking about the importance of forgiveness. She then told about the day she received a terrible telephone call. She learned that her younger sister had been brutally murdered by an axe murderer. She said she felt her world fall apart. She was in despair—this was her little sister whom she loved so much.

At the same time she thought about this horror happening to her sister, she felt an indescribable hatred rising up inside her, like a giant, towards the murderer. But at the very same moment the hatred was rising up, the Holy Spirit was leaping inside her even higher. The Holy Spirit whispered, "Forgive him, forgive him, forgive him." She knew the voice of the Holy Spirit and she knew what she had to do. There and then, while she was still on the phone, she chose to forgive the man who had so brutally killed her sister.

Enormous relief went through her whole body, because she knew she was not able to carry this horrible hatred. There and then she received the peace of God that surpasses all understanding

In the middle of the worst time of her life she experienced supernatural peace.

When I heard her telling this story, I didn't just admire her; I can't describe with words the respect I felt for her. My perception of preachers' wives changed from then on. I only then understood that we all have a story, we all have our trials and tribulations, no matter what background we come from or no matter how we look like on the outside.

In this book I feel almost as though I have stripped myself naked. I have been completely honest, maybe to some people's embarrassment. But I have done all this to be able to reach you where you are. Today I am a preacher as well, and I am happily married, I am a senior pastor with my husband Ray, and we have a lovely home together. As I travel the world together with my husband and share my testimony, I can see light in people's eyes, the light of hope.

Dear reader, I pray that reading my story will help you to see that God can take anyone, no matter their background, and heal, deliver, and restore them. If you have gone through trauma that you feel is too painful to ever get over, I want to tell you that God can heal you if you will let him.

God loves you so much that he gave His Son to die for you. Hundreds of years before Jesus came to earth, it was prophesied what Jesus would do.

Isaiah 53 says,
"Surely he took up our infirmities and carried our sorrows,
yet we considered him stricken by God,
smitten by him, and afflicted.

But he was pierced for our transgressions,

he was crushed for our iniquities;
the punishment that brought us peace was upon him,
and by his wounds we are healed. (NIV)

All you need to do is to receive Jesus Christ into your life as Lord and Saviour.

You can pray right now as you are reading:

Dear God, I believe that Jesus is your son, I believe that Jesus arose from the dead. I ask you to forgive me for all my sins. Right now I receive you into my life as my Lord and my Saviour. I ask you to heal me, just like you did for Laila. I know, God, that you have no favourites. Thank you, Lord. Amen

I hope and pray that this book has helped you to see that there is a way out of the darkness. And that the way out is through Jesus. God bless you on your journey.

Yours sincerely,

Laila

You can like to write to Laila
at the address below

The Kings Church
71 Lower Dock Street
Newport
South Wales, UK
NP20 1EH

or you can email her at
admin@kings-church.org.uk

www.kings-church.org.uk